for Roz,
and all of the Roz's
everywhere

WLRH's Sundial Writers Corner:
The Voice of the Tennessee Valley

This is the Tennessee Valley: home of both America's Rocket City and the River City. We are home to Alabama's largest city and a lot of places so small you ain't even heard of them yet. And, yes, we are a city of PhDs who say ain't and y'all.

Since 1984, Huntsville's WLRH public radio station has given local writers three minutes every Monday morning to read whatever we chose. Three minutes, times fifty-two weeks, to show you what life means in this very beautiful Tennessee Valley in this very vivid year of 2021.

These are our stories. We are the boy who felt the world change when Yuri Gagarin left the Earth. We are the wild boys from the hills who thought parrots were painted pigeons. We are the Madison teenager who is Indian in appearance but All-American as she travels the world. And much, much more.

Thank you, Dorrie Nutt and Brett Tannehill, and WLRH, for letting us show what we are here and now. Thank you, readers, for hearing us. By taking what has come out of our hearts into your own hearts, you have rubbed life into forty-two Velveteen rabbits, and we are more grateful for this life you have given us than we can show.

Michael Guillebeau, Senior Editor

52 Weeks of Sun
2021

WLRH's Sundial Writers Corner

Michael Guillebeau, Senior Editor
Associate Editors:
Pamala Dempsey
Patricia Guillebeau
Sarah Sledge

Madison Press
Madison, Alabama

Published by Madison Press
Madison, Alabama
madisonpresspublisher@gmail.com

Cover Design by Devona Hawkins
Cover Photo by Devona Hawkins

REL1030120022

52 Weeks of Sun: 1st ed.
ISBN: 978-1-7354022-5-3

Table of Contents

Rosalind Fellwock
Two Men and a Hospital Gift Cart
Kathryn Tucker Windham
The Red Scooter

January 4:
Anna Lee

My late husband Mickey and I moved to Huntsville in 1980, after he completed law school at The University of Alabama. Here in HSV, I joined seven other young

mothers to form a group of sisterly writers. We continue to gather and support each other in writing and living.

My first time on WLRH was to read a piece about our late cat, Lightning. Judy Watters' husband Harry said it made him cry. One of my best reviews.

I'm still not prolific, but I have written for *Old Huntsville* magazine, local publications and in *Hints From Heloise!*

I am grateful for my connection to WLRH. It really is like a family, and I'm glad to be part of it.

My Brief but Spectacular Take On...

The marriage proposal. I don't understand why the custom of a man proposing to a woman is still so prevalent today.

In the old days, when a man proposed marriage, he was promising that he could support a wife and their children. These days, a woman can have a child without a husband, buy a house without a husband, and fully support herself without a husband.

Yet, we still see women squealing in delight, their hands to their mouths, looking at a man down on one knee, usually with a ring in a small open box. On the news, we see engagements for women celebrities worth millions; they could buy and sell him; but yet they waited for HIM to make the move.

It seems to me the traditional proposal can become almost a distancing convention: the man, hopeful and apprehensive; the woman patient and anxious, trying to agree. More sensible might it be, for the couple to mutually allow the subject to arise naturally as an extension of their relationship and thus to enjoy the deeper significance.

I do know some couples who are now in a solid marriage, where the woman actually first proposed to the man. Some others, where they just began to talk and found they had a mutual wish to be joined. It seems to have worked well for them.

Birthdays

My mother's recent birthday, the one where she turned 100 years old, brought joy and gratitude to my whole family. She is still happy and healthy, caring and compassionate. She is a beloved figure.

Mother's birthday is easy to remember; it's a double date, 11/11. She was born on Armistice Day, now called Veterans Day. She shares her birthday month with ALL of her granddaughters. Yes, every single one of them was born in November, and now we have a little great-granddaughter who shares HER birthday with one of the others.

June is a special month, too. My parents were married in June, and I was born on their first anniversary. We have two grandsons born on the same day in June.

As for sons-in-law, we just have to remember their birthday month, because all of those who married into our family were born on the 30th day of the month.

In addition to Mother's double birth date of 11/11, all of the grandchildren married someone who also has a double birth date: 2/2 (February 2nd), 5/5 (Cinco de Mayo on May 5), and 6/6 (June 6th).

I once read mathematicians calculate that in a group of 30, the probability of two persons sharing a birthday is 70%. Well, my family has proved that theory. And we've done it TWICE!

Why I Wrote This

My mother, who is now 101, always sends greeting cards for all occasions—birthdays, Easter, Halloween, St Patrick's Day. Our whole family enjoys our celebrations, especially now that we have scattered to seven states. We always talk about birthdays and honor them. One day it occurred to me that there is an underlying pattern, so I wrote about it. Looking back at all the family times, I realize that not all of them were good, but some of them were perfect.

© 2021 Anna Lee

January 11:
Sara Leibold

I was born and raised in North Alabama, but after college I was eager to leave and see the world. I chose to forgo the traditional path and instead blaze my own

trail. My alternative nomadic lifestyle has had me working seasonally all across the country from ski resorts to the Forest Service to a bear viewing company in Alaska, and much more. When I am not working I am off traveling abroad or partaking in long distance adventures like thru-hiking the Appalachian Trail, rowing the Mississippi River, and bikepacking around Europe. I share my journeys on my adventure travel website www.whereintheworldissara.com and YouTube channel.

My Brief but Spectacular Take On...

Folks who attempt a thru-hike of the Appalachian Trail with a purist philosophy to walk the entire Appalachian mountain range ought to look further South than Springer Mountain in Georgia. Located near the small town of Weogufka in the center of Alabama, Flagg Mountain rises just over 1000ft and is recognized as the southernmost mountain in the Appalachian range, thus indicating the beginning of the Appalachians. That's why I would like to see the Appalachian Trail Conservancy, the non-profit organization acting as stewards to protect and conserve the trail, extend the world's longest hiking-only footpath a few extra hundred miles to make Flagg Mountain the official Southern Terminus of the Appalachian Trail. As of now, one can connect to Springer Mountain from Flagg Mountain by hiking the Pinhoti Trail and a section of the Benton MacKaye Trail, but there are considerable sections of unpleasant road walking. The Appalachian Trail holds a special place in my heart, and I would love to see more land protected and the trail extend to cover more of the range for future generations to enjoy.

Turkey Tracks

I follow turkey tracks
where acorns fall and smack
under looming long leaf pines
all along the endless ridge-line.

I came up with that first line while hiking the Pinhoti
Trail.
Then later, wrapped in my sleeping bag inside a cozy
two person tent,
I workshopped the rest of the poem under the light
of my headlamp.

It became my mantra while on trail.
I repeated it over and over, acting as a catalyst to
bring myself back to the present.
Now, you might think, how could you not be pre-
sent while actively hiking up and down mountains,
crossing streams, and climbing over fallen trees,
but when you hike eight plus hours a day, every day
for weeks on end,
your mind tends to wander.
I daydream to distract myself from the monotony.

But I went to the woods for connection, for chal-
lenge, for escapement
and didn't want it to be a blur.
So repeating turkey tracks would bring me back to
the moment.

I'd focus on the flora along the trail,
such as the mountain laurel slicks and
the evergreen tunnels so thick with rhododendron I
had to duck my head to pass through,
acting as gatekeepers to the Southern Appalachian
mountains.
I told myself I must return when they are in bloom
to see the whole forest in fuchsia.

I'd stop occasionally and listen to the absolute still-
ness and quiet of the woods and wonder how far
away the nearest human was, feeling as though I had
the whole wilderness to myself.
Other times I'd halt in my tracks to hear leaves
crunching as an animal scurries away in the distance,
and depending on how loud the crunching was gave
me an indication of how large the animal was. Alt-
hough most of the time it was just a squirrel making
as much of a racket as a doe.

I'd play the game stick or snake? trying to guess what
was lying on the trail in the distance, cause roots
look mighty similar to snakes laying across the path.
But it was almost always a stick.
..The snakes I usually didn't see until I was just about
to step on them.

It is above all else a privilege to be able to escape to
the woods. And escape I did.
However, the moment I stepped foot on the trail at

Flagg Mountain I felt an overwhelming feeling of be-
ing right where I was supposed to be, like the feeling
of returning home...
where acorns fall and smack
under looming long leaf pines.

Why I Wrote This

After a stressful period of time working for the census in the summer of 2020, I escaped to the woods of my home state's long trail to decompress. Thus, during my thru-hike of the Pinhoti Trail is when and where I wrote the mantra I share in "Turkey Tracks." Over the course of a few weeks and hundreds of miles, I added a sentence here or there, writing in my tent at night. Later that winter I decided to finally follow through with a personal goal of submitting a piece to the *Sundial Writers Corner*, but I struggled deciding what topic to write on. Most of my writing details grand adventures spanning weeks or months, but that would be too much information for a short story. Instead I was inspired to focus on a simple moment within the adventure when I remembered the mantra I had recently written on trail. The words started flowing from there and that's how "Turkey Tracks" came to be. My experience with the *Sundial Writers Corner* was lovely, and I hope to submit many more pieces in the future.

January 18:
Joyce Billingsley

I had the good fortune to grow up in Yorkshire, England, in a very stable family. Marrying an American soldier created a complete turn in the road and a mul-

titude of blessings. For the next twelve years we traveled around the globe and had two daughters among war and separations. Every experience made me resilient and mostly optimistic. I like to say that it was never boring and, even on my own now, I especially appreciate family. I realized along the way that life stories mustn't be lost so I started to write down those I've gathered. Everyone has stories and if reading or hearing any of mine make people remember and value their own then I've succeeded.

My Brief but Spectacular Take On...

I'm just happy to be here. Gratitude says it all... As old age creeps up on me I realize how spectacularly lucky I've been and how precious my family and friends are. I feel I have a very rich inner life built on my lifetime of experiences. I love the beauty of nature. Watching the sun rise is an emotional experience for me. Music astounds me. Humanity has created so much quality all around us we just have to recognize and appreciate it. I strongly believe in intuition. I always listen to my inner voice and it's never failed me.

The Allotment

In the summer of 1969 Mum and Dad moved into what was to be their last home. It was a bungalow near Cottingley Bridge. Dad had just turned 61 and Mum was almost 59. We daughters were grown and gone so they'd left the big house and garden at Stoney Ridge. It was time for them to do less work and enjoy an easier life.

The house had a small garden and a greenhouse. They methodically moved just a few perennials from their old house to the new. They planted a pink climbing rose over the big kitchen window and a hydrangea next to the French door into the lounge. They scattered cottage garden favorites like columbine and nasturtiums in the borders and a weeping cherry in the center circular flowerbed. The back garden soon acquired a couple of apple trees and a smattering of phlox and yellow poppies. Dad filled the greenhouse with dahlias, tomato plants and a grapevine. By then he'd run out of room.

Fortunately, there were allotments nearby that opened the door for many more possibilities.

These weren't mere Victory Gardens that came into being for the First World War. Its history began during the Middle Ages, as the village of Bingley grew, it became the middens where sewage and other waste was dumped. That on top of the Ice Age's glacial deposits went into creating very fertile, productive soil.

In October of 1844 Lady Ferrand, who owned the land, made it available to the community. A ceremony took place in which Benjamin Disraeli officially opened the allotments to the public. Not yet Prime Minister, he and Lord Ferrand shared similar political views. Disraeli was a guest at their residence, Harden Grange. He also played an entertaining game of cricket, one of the celebratory events of that day.

By 1919 the movers and shakers among the allotment renters decided to incorporate and took steps to buy the land from the Ferrands. This was successfully accomplished and recorded on 10 November of that year. They offered shares that people could purchase so that many tenants could now claim ownership and thus was born the Cottingley Bridge Allotment Gardens comprising over a hundred separate plots, a vast area stretching across the river valley.

By the spring of 1970 dad was officially the tenant of allotment plot 7b paying a mere ten pounds a year rent, literally dirt cheap—and he worked it for the next 20 years. It was close to the entrance and was bordered by the river. There was a water pump, an old greenhouse and the remains of a tumbling down wooden shed. It was an easy five-minute bicycle ride from home on Hazel Beck, along Beckfoot Lane, coast over the foot bridge and turn left at the red phone box to arrive at his sanctuary. To dad it was perfect. If he even knew its history, I'm pretty sure he took it for granted. He was just happy to have a place to go. Not least for the company of fellow gardeners. There was always someone to talk to, someone to commiserate with over the slug or greenfly infestations. Mum would pack him a sandwich so he could stay longer. He also kept a saltshaker in the greenhouse to eat his tomatoes. He was a regular at the gardens for 20 years, sometimes staying most of the day.

In the mid 70's, there were years with unusually hot, dry summers. Waiting for rain wasn't an option, dad had to go to water every day. I went there a few times but only in the summer when he proudly showed me his produce. Mostly it leaned heavily on lettuces, onions, rhubarb and raspberries in summer and brussels sprouts and cabbages in the winter. My daughters remember how their grandpa would pluck peapods off the vine and popping them open with his big broad thumb he'd offer them. "Ooooh lovely, try summa these."

Dad surrendered his garden plot in 1990 due to ill health and I'm sure all the people he spent time with there are long gone now. The corporation, begun in part by the Marshall family who have been involved since its inception, is still active to this day. Challenged by disastrous flooding in 2015 the tenants and shareholders have had to spend considerable effort and money to shore up the riverbank, restore the paths and roadways, dispose of tons of rubbish deposited by the floodwaters and bring in many tons more of topsoil. And in 2019 the group put out a commemorative booklet celebrating the allotments' centenary.

In my mind's eye now, I visualize the evening fog rising from the river shrouding the many past tenants, old rustics making ghostly patrols at night, roaming along the paths to see that their gardens are still being tended as they'd expect. Their stewardship is over but the allotments are still in good hands for many more generations to come.

Why I Wrote This

It started when I saw a wallpaper pattern named The Allotments in a magazine. It had a greenhouse repeating prominently which reminded me of my father's plot. I felt something magical happened that motivated me. Researching it on the internet I discovered the organization and contacted the secretary. He offered to send me the centenary booklet with its history. It was a treasure trove of information. I plucked out that nugget from history about its grand opening and I was off and running with it. I love to connect my family to the past and this was the perfect avenue.

January 25:
Andrew V. Gonzales

Hello! My name is Andrew V Gonzales and I currently (as of writing this biography) live, work, and play in Huntsville, AL. I earn a roof over my head as

an analyst by day and stave off the specter of middle age by night. Pizza, public radio, and local markets are my love language. Co-existing with our planet is my life and I have weathered grocery totes, boxes of glass bottles, a compost bin, and solar panels to prove it. When I'm not indulging or saving the world, I am documenting my life, writing, or (my newest love) reading.

My Brief but Spectacular Take On...

Purpose. For years, I've been searching for my purpose in life. I've looked through lenses, searched on stages, and even thought I found it on a ballot. With each new pursuit, I gained new skills and met inspiring people. I was placed in situations that pushed me beyond my comfort zone into growth. At the same time, however, I never escaped the perpetual rule of doubt, worry, and anxiety. They ended every search. If I wasn't experiencing uninterrupted bliss throughout my pursuit, then the pursuit was not my purpose. Furthermore, if I was not living my purpose, I was wasting my time. Every end was a new beginning and every moment not devoted to the search was retasked. This monument to immaturity was torn down by a set of words I wrote after an evening of rumination while washing the dishes: "Don't become so obsessed with finding your purpose in life that you forget to live it." (Passenger 86:2). The next day, after I committed those words to writing, I stopped searching. I wanted happiness and I already knew where to look. It wasn't anywhere near purpose. Maybe purpose itself was an attribute of immaturity.

Sunday School #46

The past month, I have been doing my duty and remaining home in an effort to prevent the spread of the pandemic we now find ourselves in.

I, fortunately, work from home. I, mostly, eat at home. And I, happily, stay busy at home.

I stay busy at home catching up on the to-do list that preceded this unprecedented event. Long-standing logistical and organizational tasks populated most of it. Add in a much-needed website overhaul (thanks for noticing) and the result nearly equals today minus work on new content. It, the new content, is what I'm most excited for. They are journal excerpts from my very first journal!

Exciting (and embarrassing) as they are, reading through such old accounts takes a substantial amount of time. They also evoke many long-forgotten emotions of events and peoples past. I underestimated their effect. Upon reflection of my first journal in my current one, I found myself trying to induce some inspired lesson on treading this delicate threshold. Instead, I learned something else.

"Standard day, yesterday. My walk was lovely as was lunch. I wrote a lot yet my last page from yesterday's entry was very forced and not quite genuine. I must have been trying to write a Sunday School. I can't make a Sunday School happen in

here. It just happens (like now). I have no control over it."
— Referendum 36:7

What I love most about learning (and this series) is also what I hate most about it: I cannot force it. Learning from the mistakes of others has long been a mainstay of mine and a preventative measure against embarrassment and failure. However, it is the very premise of failure that teaches me most.

A lesson not learned from my own mistake is a lesson not learned at all.

Where do you learn your lessons from?

Here's to a lifelong series of mistakes.

Why I Wrote This

This essay is the forty-sixth instantiation of a writing series I called, "Sunday School". Every Sunday, for two years straight, I would read back at a week's worth of journal entries, find the verse (or verses) that spoke most to me, and write about it (or them) on my blog. Each essay included the inspiring verse(s) such that it read seamlessly. Sunday School #46 was inspired by the not-so-glamorous exercise of organizing entries from my very first journal and the difficulties associated with upholding the series itself.

February 1:
Susan Hazen Guthrie

Susan Hazen Guthrie is a Stage Director and Teaching Artist, working extensively in Shakespeare, chore-ography, fight choreography, and performance. She is a Master Teacher of voice and speech, language and verse literature, and a curriculum specialist. She directed and consulted for the *Alabama Shakespeare Festival.* She is the author and lead artist of *Shakespeare in the Classroom.* Ms. Guthrie lectures nationwide for the NEA and The Poetry Foundation: POETRY OUT LOUD. She is a member of Alabama's Coweeta Poets, and is most recently published in the August issue #35 of *The Rose in the World* magazine.

My Brief but Spectacular Take On...

Nobility – concept of another time, but often coming to mind; probably because I'm immersed in Shakespeare – sharing poetry with all people. In common with all people, images of knights, jousts, crusades, come to mind at the mention of, "nobility." In drama, I ask, "Where would I find these characters today?"

Where is nobility today?

If Nobles past, lived a vow to the death, to house and protect people of their land – within castle walls and outward community; if in exchange for family autonomy, nobility endowed king and country – how does that translate to wealth, strength, and education today?

Protecting the weak, innocent; welcoming the stranger, comforting the sick; contributing wealth, strength, education through a republic made equal – this is noble. It is also the American heart.

Heartsick I am, today, as I consider the structure of everything I see – horde within castle walls, suspicion anything with good grammar, cheat country; wealth is the only strength, and there can only ever be one winner.

I know my hatred and the belief on which it stands is equidistant from the truth as mine enemy's. For now that is all I have to catch a breath, remember my God and country, and be ruled by love. There is nobility in that tiny stronghold in my American heart. I believe there are more like me.

Oh, Kitchen Floor

The dark wood of the kitchen floor holds many secrets.
All the dust, cat food crumbs, unbelief, and water spots
are hidden to the eye, unmoved by the routine,
saved for the schedule; and, thank God, deniable (?)
These cracks in perfection remain secret, surer than sin,
Until those 20 mins of the day – those 10-20 minutes when the sun
reveals the cat hair – the great and fertile fields of cat hair
and such, that CANNOT be quickly swept up by the lick
and a promise of the radius of a human arm
holding a dampened paper towel of slinging sink droplets
compassing to catch this sin of neglect
or rather the shrinking 25th hour
or the lie of Mr. Clean
or time.

I stand still wondering why I am surprised
and why I believed my effort and standard would sustain.
God must be in His Heaven.
He certainly is not here in my kitchen.
There is only surrender to dust and time,
and so I wonder, if I left dust, would it accumulate
into a man? Would dust, over time,
swirl up into a figure and down again –
eventually scatter across the floor?
How many mighty ones are here in pieces,
in increments, in cells?
Of course company takes philosophy to joy.
Holiday droppings will join the floor's daily collections,
and I accept Creation's life and death;
and hope the inevitable dark will strengthen my light.

Why I Wrote This

The concept of my house as clean is shattered twice a day when the angle of the sun on its way up and then later on its way down, reveals what is actually on the floor — hidden the other 23 hours and 40 minutes of the day by the grain and the dark, but, nevertheless, on the floor, always. And, as always, thoughts chain through presence of missing the Martha-Stewart-mark and doubting home-owner-house-keeper wor-thiness-ness.

On this particular pre-Thanksgiving, preparations for feast and family – thrilling, indeed, were second to determination for a thoroughly clean house – thrilling the generations of moms and sisters current and gone before. Indeed! And, indeed, the poem turns to consider all the *befores*, before me in the all of *alls*.

A blue jay just lighted on the arm of a leafy lawn chair. I must go write a poem about it…

© 2021 Susan Hazen Guthrie

February 8:
Monita Soni

With one foot in Huntsville, the other in India and a heart steeped in humanity, writing is a contemplative practice. Borrowing a tweet from a red cardinal, the

wind whistling through green meadows, a child's laughter, a twinkle from fireflies, I weave poems. Nature has given me an outline of my own masterpiece. I delight in writing and coloring on my notepad. I write, rewrite and write some more. The more I write, the more I fall in love with the craft. The stories I hear, read and recount embody me...like old friends, bedazzled with the blessings.

My Brief but Spectacular Take On...

I was born in Chandigarh, a flourishing model city designed by the Swiss-French modernist architect *Le Corbusier*. My childhood was glorious. With deep appreciation, I unravel the sacred thread of memory. It was an all-inclusive care package. An aesthetically designed home. Warm, caring parents. Gourmet family meals, Music, engaging conversations, piping hot *parathas*, pies, custards, cakes and ice cream. Laughter. A lot of laughter. I finished my schoolwork in recess or on the *rickshaw/tonga* ride home. The long afternoons became more abundant with an endless supply of story books, and poetry. When I was married, my environment became transactional. As an escape, I became engrossed in my medical career but missed my parents acutely. Soon my children took center stage. I immersed myself in recreating a magical childhood for them. But my birth-star propelled me overseas. I had to live away from my roots, heritage and family. I trained, retrained and set up my laboratory. My mother stayed with me for over two months and helped me in establishing my medical practice in Decatur, Alabama. But when my dad started calling her three times a day, I sent her back to him in India. The separation from my family created a yearning that broke my heart open. I missed them every moment. Everything simple and seemingly ordinary was gilded with their selfless love and affection for me. This is a recurring theme in my stories.

An Ode to a Broom

Cleanliness is the emblem of a pure mind.

We lived in Chembur, a suburb of Bombay, the financial and Bollywood capital of India. I studied at St.Anthony's high school. On weekends we took a trip to buy groceries at the amazing *Chandan* stores. There were so many mouth-watering delicacies in glass jars on the counter but my mom bought me the same treat every week. The smallest bar of Cadbury Milk Chocolate, locally made from the Chocolate factory Bombay. It was a five minute-drive but we walked back home. Mom held two bags and I held the one with the two chocolate bars wrapped in purple and silver. One for me and one for my sister. I waited patiently for this long walk every week because the reward was sweet. One day Mom bought a broom. She asked me to carry it. I was mortified! I might run into some mean boys from the adjacent boys' school. They were notorious! Those boys from *OLPS*. They would tease me forever! *I can't do that*, I told her. *Alright,* her tone was sedate and blithe. *If you are embarrassed by carrying the jhadoo, we can walk apart.* So I did. But the sight of her elegantly draped in a pink Bombay Dyeing saree with a vintage broom tucked in her grocery bag has stayed with me.

My mother is a regal being. An incarnation of *Annapurna,* the Goddess of perpetual nourishment. Her home, hearth and purse are ever abundant. Mother always had help for domestic chores but she valued dignity of labor. She swept with Emily Dickinson's many-colored brooms, keeping her home, garden and mind free of dust and prejudice. Purple, amber brooms swept up radiant sunsets. She conjured magic to pluck twinkling stars from the sky. *Cleanliness is akin to Godliness* is her motto.

On that *jhadoo-day*, no one witnessed my predicament, especially those mean boys! This memory was tucked away in the recesses of consciousness. When I moved to America, like many others, I bought a broom and a vacuum cleaner. Cleaning does not come naturally to me but I manage. Last year before COVID, I hired a lady from Thailand to clean my house. She brought a broom identical to the one we had procured from the *Chandan* Stores in Bombay. Within minutes she had cleaned my apartment with that single broom. I was overcome with joy to find the same "Indian" broom at Patel Brothers, Indian grocery store in Atlanta. This time without hesitation and to my daughter's chagrin, I carried the broom with alacrity! Now, *jhadoo* is an important member of my broom closet. Slender, straight and light, she does not doze off but prattles away to dusters, swiffers and mops.

Every morning when I sweep my kitchen, I hold the broom in my hand. It is so easy now to clean corners and crevices of my home. Her flexible grassy reeds gently lift molecules of dust, lurking insects, snippets of haikus and palindromes. When I survey my clean floors, walls and ceilings, my heart swells with pride. Not due to my education or vocation but despite it. As I sweep, I become my mother's maid:

Wise, foolish, weak and strong all at once. This humble broom, like many murmuring memories: flickering candles, songbirds, scented kerchiefs, embroidered frocks, handmade dolls, spices, warm porridge and the swing on her yellow rain tree has magic. The magic whisks and whirls me back to the bountiful bowers of childhood and to my sweet mother.

Why I Wrote This

The COVID- 19 pandemic forced us to stay indoors. Clean. Cull. Organize and take account of our lives. Remove both external and internal clutter. One day, while sweeping my kitchen floor, I was reminded of how clean my mother's living space was. Spotless. Neat. Immaculate. A place of worship. I laughed out loud at the memory of our trip to the grocery store, when Mom asked me to carry a broom. I objected then. But now I hold the broom with love in my hands and sweep my floors. Every movement brings me closer to my mother. I wonder what my grandson would do when faced with a similar request? Well... that's another story.

February 15:
Patrick W. Lappert

My name is Patrick W. Lappert. I have always included my middle initial because it represents my father's name, and being third-born, I have always treas-ured it as a sign of my father's love for me, and of his confidence in me. I was born in Caracas, Venezuela. That is where my parents met. He was a Jewish war refugee who had served as a French Cavalry officer, but had to flee to South America when the Vichy were given control by their Nazi masters. My mother, born in London, had been conscripted into the foreign service, served in Cashmere, India during the war, and was posted to the British Consulate in Caracas at war's end. They had four children.

I grew up in San Francisco in the 60s, but dropped out of High School and left home just after my sixteenth birthday. I spent four years living on a sailboat, and adventuring around San Francisco Bay, while working in various jobs. Eventually I returned to school, and by a series of ridiculous, and providential circumstances, completed my MD degree. I am board certified in General Surgery, and Plastic/ Reconstructive Surgery. At the same time, I was commissioned an officer in the Navy, and served for twenty-four years, retiring with the rank of Captain. For three of those years, I flew fighter aircraft with the United States Marine Corps.

My wife and I have been married for forty years and have raised six children. I started life as a Jewish kid, lived most of my life as a rabid atheist, convinced that scientific materialism can understand everything, and am now ordained clergy in the Roman Catholic Church.

Substitution

Russell and the boy walked on,
in steady pace, the many blocks from where the rattling bus
had left them.
The avenues of the city, where the houses shoulder together,
was where Dan lived. Russell's faithful Army brother
lately returned from Viet Nam.

Russell had refused a rifle, and so was sent to care
for boys whose blood he'd stanched, and gaping wounds had
dressed.
His voice, though from New York, did not bear hint of impatience,
but rather the calm, and reassurance of the ones who
embrace the dying with tender care.

And Dan had also been a medic;
had come to bring relief to Russell.
Had sent him home to safety.
His substitute.

Russell smoked his unfiltered Lucky Strike.
As they waited for the light to change,
he knocked the ember from its end, and without thought,
stripped the paper from the leaf and compressed it
to invisibility. No trace for the enemy that he had paused a while to
rest.

The hundred small habits that cling to men who
daily walk along the very edges of life,
and do not trust the smallest change,
that might undo them.

A pilgrimage to pay respect,
to a holy brotherhood of men who love each other,
without the least stain of corrupt desires or use.
To speak few words, yet tell in full the breadth of unalloyed love.

To place, in sacred trust, one's very life if the evil should spring
suddenly
from whatever hide, or stealth it had prepared.
To substitute for a friend imperiled,
and let him live another day.

The pace had slowed in the mild fatigue of the distance.
Another block of homes to pass;
the slowing sound of a car approached their quarter,
as if to park. The faintest crunching of the tires on gutter grit,
and the sound of an electric window opening on the sea green car.

It had the length and crushed velour of counterfeit wealth.
The passenger in coat and tie all paisley. A war of colors waged on
the corpulent abdomen of the man who turned to them and spoke.
His words were low, and could not be reckoned, except they ended
with the inflection of a question or request.
So, Russell stopped, and turned to help.

The boy just behind his friend, now saw the man's face:
a pale mass of lumps and creases,
topped with hair like thick straw soaked in oil.
His eyes like holes, framed in the squint of malevolent pleasure.
Suddenly presenting his fat right hand, a signet of gold on the
shortest
of his fingers, wrapped around the grip,
of a snubbed nose revolver, its muzzle half a yard
from Russell's face.

The flow of time which they'd been measuring
in the pace of their walk was now lengthened to the point of still-
ness,
deathly stillness.
No thought.
No question.
No hesitation to weigh and measure the possible result.
He grasped his friend by the shoulder seams of his

brown suede jacket, and in one great pull spun him 'round,
and placed himself between, feeling the presence of the pistol at his
back.

Now pushing, pushing, pushing him
into the alcove entrance of one of the narrow homes.
The car squealed away as the occupants laughed,
as men laugh when they've too long filled their cups
with bitterness.

He learned that day that he'd been given a precious gift.
Not sought, but placed secretly there
when his infant heart was being knit,
first in image, then in flesh.
The moment had revealed it.
A gift when placed, now gift again when felt
in sudden, infinite strength of love,
for a dearest brother.

His boyhood had in that instant ended,
not in a moment hidden and carnal,
but in an unexpected rush of virtue.

So many years ago, yet still beside him somehow.
His name in the litany of his prayers, though now imploring rest,
for so great a friend, who'd steered to gentleness and patience,
the boy who is now grown old.
Who in the cold air of morning still knocks the ember
from the Lucky Strike, and strips the paper;
the tiny leaves falling like a precious, private autumn
that love has made invisible to the enemy.

Why I Wrote This

I've only recently begun to write from my life's experience, and this piece is my first. It is an important moment in my life because of something I had missed in childhood. I had, for years, looked forward to my Bar Mitzvah. That day was denied me because of my parent's divorce. That catastrophe was an unbearable addition to the weight of doubts that I would ever be man enough. It is an account of the last day of my boyhood; my Bar Mitzvah.

© 2021 Patrick W. Lappert

February 22:
Rose Battle

I was born into a very large family. My father had nine siblings and my mother had seven. They married. We had an army of support growing up in the home our

father built for us in the woods on "Battle Hill" near Birmingham.

Our Battle family's life was centered on sports and politics. Our home life included our parents and the four of us children: Rose, Joe, Bill and Ginnie Battle, and our horse, monkey, dog and rooster.

All my life, I've written poems and stories for myself, and written and illustrated stories for the many

children in our family. I've told stories about "Battle Hill" in the 1940s and 1950s, as well as "Granny Stories" about our mother's mother. I do this to preserve our joys, our Southern ways, and words.

Nine years ago, I began being on WEUP Radio on "The 50 Yard Line," a call-in sports show.

Thirteen years ago, I first tried out to be on WLRH Public Radio. I've loved telling my stories on the *Sundial Writers Corner*. It has led me to many opportunities to achieve my goal of sharing the great parts of growing up Southern.

My father would reply to any idea I had by saying, "Throw it out there, Sister Baby. Let's see if you have any takers."

So I have, and I am.

You'uns Has Painted You'un's Pigeons, Ain't You'uns?

When most of Granny Troxell's eight children had flown the coop in the late 1930s, our Great-Uncle Garl decided he would bring Granny a gift of a parrot. Granny, her sister Aunt Ackie, and her life-long best friend Vash Ti, ran Granny's household in the small town of Bridgeport, AL.

The new parrot, "Miz Molly," was placed in a large cage on Granny's back porch each day. Across the clothesline and garden lived Mrs. McCorkey. She and Granny would run out and yell, "Yoo hoo!!" to each other when new gossip hit Bridgeport. Miz Molly soon caught on and began yelling "Yoo hoo" to copy Granny. After much running back and forth to their porches, the two ladies had to rig up a bell and forego "Yoo hooing!"

Aunt Akie was born blind, but she loved to walk several blocks from Granny's to her other sister Aunt Kate's house. She used her cane and sang, "Froggie Went A' Courting" on the way as she passed under the bridge on her walk.

That did not keep the little Gilley boys from teasing her, trying to trip her, and being scamps. Aunt Ackie would kindly try to teach them manners to no avail.

One day she said, "If you rapscallions behave, I'll let y'all meet our bird, 'Miz Molly.' You have to show me for one month you can behave, then we will have you over for cake, a Co-Cola, and to meet our bird."

By the very hardest, the Gilley boys were acceptably acting O.K. for a whole month of summer.

The great day came!

Aunt Akie grated a coconut for the coconut cake that Granny baked. Vash-Ti walked to Aunt Evelyn's pharmacy for 6 Co-Colas. Matt Todd delivered a block of ice cream. Miz Molly was moved in her cage into the dining room and the great occasion was all ready to begin.

Granny removed the Gilley boys' little grimey hats, invited them to wash their hands in the kitchen sink and sit at the dining table. Aunt Akie said the blessing as they all held hands. Vash-Ti removed the shawl covering Miz Molly and the parrot shone in all of her radiant glory.

One of the little Gilley boys yelled out at the top of his lungs:

"Why Miz Troxell, you'uns has painted you'un's pigeons, ain't you'uns?"

© 2021 Rose Battle

March 1:
John S. Mebane

I am Professor Emeritus of English at the University of Alabama in Huntsville. Originally a specialist in Renaissance literature and culture, especially Shakespeare, I have also pursued interdisciplinary studies in religion and warfare, focusing upon the conflicts among pagan heroic ideals and Christian ideas concerning pacifism and principles of justice in warfare. My interest in this topic stems in part from my experience in combat in Viet Nam and Cambodia in 1969-70. I've published two books and a number of articles. I earned a bachelor's degree from Presbyterian College and a Ph. D. from Emory University.

My Brief but Spectacular Take On...

When I was drafted in 1968, I had spent altogether too little time contemplating the rationale for the war in Viet Nam. After serving in combat in the 11th Armored Cavalry, I began to contemplate not only our involvement in Viet Nam, but warfare in general. For a while after returning home I tried to avoid thinking about the war, and I immersed myself in the study of English literature, especially Shakespeare. Shakespeare, I soon learned, dramatized warfare in ways that led his audiences to contemplate and analyze the moral, political and religious dimensions of war. He doesn't always lead us toward an obvious conclusion about these issues, but he does lead us to become deeply engaged with them. Eventually I developed, with the assistance of colleagues in political science and philosophy, a course with the grandiose title "Literature, Religion, and Warfare." After decades of immersion in these questions, I find that the theorist of warfare with whom I identify most closely is Erasmus of Rotterdam, who is not quite a complete pacifist, but who argues — persuasively, in my judgment — that beginning a war is always wrong.

My Visit to Tokyo

In the spring of 1970 I visited Tokyo, Japan. I was on leave from Viet Nam, where I served in the 11th Armored Cavalry, so I was looking forward to seven days of safety. We were warned, however, that there were some dangers. One example we were given was that Japanese Communists might ask us to sign petitions that they claimed were documents advocating peace; in reality, we would be signing confessions that would identify us as war criminals. For various reasons, the way to stay safe was to team up with a buddy. I did so, but on the second day in Tokyo, my buddy came down with malaria. I took him to an American military hospital.

On my trip back from the hospital on a commuter train, I noticed a young Japanese man who was staring at me. Eventually he came up to me, bowed politely, and asked if I were an American soldier. I said "yes." He then said he had something to tell me: several members of his wife's family, he continued, were killed by the atomic bomb that the Americans had dropped 25 years earlier on the city of Nagasaki.

I froze. What could I possibly say? Fortunately, he continued by telling me that many young Japanese of his generation had become pacifists because of their experience of the war. He was grateful that Americans and Japanese of our generation could become friends.

I think I managed to say something like "yes, me too," before he bowed again and went quietly on his way.

I often wish that I could find him today and thank him. I am profoundly grateful for his expression of faith that not only individuals, but entire cultures can change, and that the act of reaching out in peaceful friendship to a stranger could contribute to that process. In recent years my memory of this gesture of peaceful good will has lifted my spirits and given me genuine comfort.

Why I Wrote This

I want to honor the commitment to peace and the courage of the young man that I encountered on the train in Tokyo in 1970. Our conversation took place approximately 25 years after the bombing of Hiroshima and Nagasaki and the end of World War II. I had grown up hearing stories about the war: I can remember my seventh-grade teacher, a widow, breaking down in tears as she spoke to us about losing someone dear to her in the war. The suffering caused by the war was so terrible that it's easy to see why it would be an immense psychological, moral, and spiritual struggle to overcome the animosities among the combatants. Yet, as I write this, I can say that reconciliation has occurred, and Americans, Germans, and Japanese have indeed become friends. This healing was possible because of the benevolence of people like the person who spoke to me on the train.

March 15:
Jimmy Robinson

I first experienced the satisfaction of hearing my own voice reading my poems and short prose on the *Sundial Writers Corner* with production master Judy Wat-

ters and have continued with current producer Dorrie Nutt. I've been writing since college at the University of Alabama where I had undergraduate poetry writing classes with Thomas Rabbit and Everett Maddox. I later studied Latin American Literature at the National Autonomous University of Mexico while living in Mexico City, hometown of my wife, Guadalupe. Returning to Huntsville I got involved with The Huntsville Literary Association's monthly poetry workshop group with whom I have met regularly for three decades now. I eventually became an assistant editor of their nationally circulated poetry magazine, *POEM*. I taught Spanish at Huntsville High and in the Department of Foreign Languages and Literatures at UAH.

My Brief but Spectacular Take On...

Education and travel. Education and travel have been two principal catalysts in my life and most of my writing. These endeavors go hand in hand, because to read and study is to travel in many ways; and to travel is to learn directly or indirectly about an unlimited array of possibilities.

These Ashes

are what little is left
After the leaves have been consumed.
A useless powder dull and gray
Only a painter, potter, or priest
Could put to any practical purpose.

There is the deeper hunger
After the great feast has been devoured,
When the guests have left,
The revelry subsided,
And the placid silence
Beyond the noise returned;
Ashes are what little is left.

Sparkling beads hurled from floats
Into crowds of uplifted hands
Lining streets in desperate celebration
Lie limp and dull amid the muck
And dangle sacrificed from sprawling oaks.

Armies of street sweepers with brooms,
Rotating bristles driven along curbs,
And recyclers handing out plastic bags
Are not enough to erase the futile festivity.
Fireworks alighting the purple night
fall dusty gray on cobblestone and cracked asphalt.

Green sprouting grass only a faint hope
Between cracks in disgruntled pavement
Where shoes stumble and trip as though lost
On what was once a clear and determined path.
After the crawfish, shrimp, rum, and wine,
There is no hunger or desire to feed the nausea.

A dry wafer, like a blank piece of paper,
And a minute sip of almost-repugnant wine
Is sufficient to sustain the solemn trudge
Across the most vast of all deserts: the one inside.

Why I Wrote This

"These Ashes" is an example of a poem that examines something physical and expands into a concept that leads to images, connections, and a conclusion the poet did not foresee at the beginning.

March 22:
Monita Soni

With one foot in Huntsville, the other in India and a heart steeped in humanity, writing is a contemplative practice. Borrowing a tweet from a red cardinal, the  wind whistling through green meadows, a child's laughter, a twinkle from fireflies, I weave poems. Nature has given me an outline of my own masterpiece. I delight in writing and coloring on my notepad. I write, rewrite and write some more. The more I write, the more I fall in love with the craft. The stories I hear, read and recount embody me...like old friends, bedazzled with the blessings.

My Brief but Spectacular Take On...

I have deep respect and adoration for my illustrious father, my patient son and my irascible grandson. But I idolize the women in my life. My elegant mother, my grandmothers with breath-taking beauty and verve, my friends from various walks of life. My sister who tirelessly took care of my sister in the last decade. My aunts who showered books, candies and handmade parkas upon me. My Moon-flower of a daughter, whose compassionate eyes, and a refined intellect illuminates my days. My teachers and their patience over my brattiness and over competitive spirit. The Goddess energy. A nurturing life force. An indomitable strength. A mountain stream. The morning light. A bird song at dusk. A dew drop. A baby's breath. A vedic hymn. A gentle touch that always soothes my overwrought nerves. I draw life enhancing energy from all the female energies in my life. In my poem, I salute them.

There's a Woman in the House

Whatever you give a woman, she will make it greater. If you give her a house, she will make it a home... William Golding

I fold the blanket, a touch smooths
The wrinkles on my hand
Her light enters through the whorls
She steps softly, her feet barely
Skimming the wild flowers
Wrapped in translucent blue

She smiles a million stars
There are butterflies in her aura
There's a woman in the house

There's a woman in the house
She rests her hand on my shoulders
Offers a drink of lemon and honey
She strolls silently in the gladioli
Her coral parasol reflecting light
Now she is peering into a lotus
Her head bent in prayer
There's a woman in the house

There's a woman in the house
Her breath rises and falls
She rests her head on my shoulder
We both read the same line
On the page of life

We hold kindness
Our eyes close...we are happy
There's a woman in the house

There's a woman in the house
 She cleans, cooks and bakes
She mends holes in my soul
Sifts thought books and papers
Finds poems I have not written
All cobwebbed worries vanish
She hums as she works
There's a woman in the house

There's a woman in the house
She wears a printed floral blouse
With a pocket that holds a key
She laughs a lot, laughs and sings
She gives the best hugs
Children bounce in and out of her lap
She paints with her eyes
There's a woman in the house

There's a woman in the house
 She's fierce, her eyes blaze
She wields a golden bow
Her gaze is steadfast
Demons dare not mock her
She keeps guard over earth
She does not sleep a blink
There's a woman in the house

There's a woman in the house
She is my grandmother in heaven
She is my mother who is still strong
She is my sister who tends to her
She is my daughter who holds my hand
She is my friend who walks with me
She wants me to call her name
There's a woman in the house.

Why I Wrote This

My daughter, Abha Soni, was furloughed from her service in Dermatopathology Laboratory in the spring of 2019. She left her apartment in Georgia and came home. Her sweet aura permeated our house in Alabama. On waking up one morning, I felt a gentle touch on my shoulder. I noticed her beautiful hands with long, delicate fingers. I was reminded of my mother's hands. Soft. Supple. Able. A sculptor's dream. How mother took my wrinkled hands in hers as soon as we met. Lamenting their dryness as she rubbed in hand cream. I told her about how my profession required frequent hand washing. Her face grew grim. I tried to steal my hands away from hers but she held on to them. The day this poem was written, I looked down at this memory and, before I knew it, my wrinkled hand (a philosopher's hand, as my father called it) had written this poem on my notepad. The lines just gushed out, as though a woman had anointed my forehead with a bottle of oil. The women in my life appeared one by one, in the glistening sheen of the rhythmic refrain.

March 29:
Sarah Bèlanger

I spent most of my childhood bouncing from state to state, but I've called North Alabama my home for the last twenty years. I am a food writer and

photographer. I was the primary author of the book *North Alabama Beer: An Intoxicating History* and am currently working on my first novel. I live with my husband and a quirky Betta fish named Milton in Madison, Alabama.

Mrs. Coleman

Throughout the years, from kindergarten to graduate school, I've had a lot of teachers. Some were good, and some were bad, but none were as memorable or eccentric as my second-grade teacher Mrs. Coleman.

I was eight years old when my family moved from the suburbs of Connecticut to rural Maine. That year, there were many changes — new house, new friends, new baby brother — and, because I moved midway through the school year, a new second-grade teacher.

I hadn't been a huge fan of my previous teacher. She was prim and proper with tidy, pinned-up hair and color-coordinating outfits. She insisted on good etiquette at all times. When answering a question, we had to stand next to our desks, not fidget, and speak in a loud, clear voice. And when asking to do something, we needed to say, "may I."

I asked, "Can I please go to the bathroom?"

She smirked and said, "I don't know. Can you?"

Being eight and having the bladder of a hamster, I hated this. But this is what happens when you have a teacher who loves rules.

Mrs. Coleman was different.

She had a loose concept of structure for us—or herself. She wore bedroom slippers to class. And during story time, she'd choose a student to brush her short, wispy hair. It was an honor to be picked.

I don't remember learning Geography, Science, or Math from Mrs. Coleman. Or History. Or Social

Studies. I did learn how to spell Hawaii. H-I, wait…
H-A? Are there three I's or just two? Never mind, I
didn't learn that either.

I'd like to think these subjects were part of the sec-
ond grade curriculum that I've forgotten. Still it is en-
tirely possible Mrs. Coleman didn't teach these sub-
jects because she didn't want to.

But she was a fabulous storyteller. She was chock-
full of interesting yet horrible anecdotes, which she
sprinkled throughout her lessons.

Did you know Beethoven's father beat him regu-
larly? I do, thanks to Mrs. Coleman. After telling us
the composer's abusive upbringing contributed to
greatness, she gave us a wistful look and shook her
head at her class's wasted potential, frittered away by
soft, liberal parenting.

One time she mentioned her first husband.

First husband? It's always surprising to find out
your teachers have lives outside of the classroom.

"What happened to him," we asked.

She shrugged. "He disappeared in Egypt."

Our mouths fell open. We peppered her with ques-
tions—why was her husband in Egypt, what hap-
pened to him, is he dead?

She sighed, annoyed to recount such a trivial story,
but finally explained he'd gotten lost while exploring
a pyramid.

Even as an adult, I wonder what the hell happened
to him. Being older and wiser, I suspect "pyramid"
was a euphemism for "mistress," and "lost" for "di-
vorced." Although I really don't know.

Unlike some other students, I loved Mrs. Coleman's eccentricities and her shocking stories. But even I admit, sometimes she went too far.

It was the day after NBC's annual airing of *The Wizard of Oz*. The entire class was excited to talk about it. We discussed the geopolitical ramifications the death of Wicked Witch of the East had on Munchkinland and how the Scarecrow symbolized the discontented American farmer of the 19th-century. Just kidding. We were second graders. We wondered if it would be fun to ride in a tornado or if flying monkeys make good pets — doubtful on both counts.

Mrs. Coleman didn't say much, but when we got to Dorothy and her ruby slippers, she chimed in. "Dorothy died of a drug overdose."

A hush fell over the class.

Of course, we were familiar with drugs. Nancy Regan's DARE program had made sure of that, but the idea that Dorothy, in her gingham dress and pigtails, died in a back alley with a syringe sticking out of her arm was appalling. Mrs. Coleman must be wrong, and I wasn't the only one who thought so.

"Dorothy's isn't dead," argued my classmate.

Staring down at the distressed child, Mrs. Coleman realized her mistake. "Oh no, dear. The actress who played Dorothy, Judy Garland, she died of a drug overdose. Pills. Such a shame." And recognizing a good teaching moment, she added, "So that's why you shouldn't do drugs, class."

What had Dorothy carried around in that basket of hers? From the sounds of it, meth.

The students were slow to process this information, but as we did little arms shot up around the room.

"What about the Scarecrow?"

"Dead. Cancer. The Lion too. Auntie Em killed herself. Quite tragic."

Dear lord, this was turning into a bloodbath.

Most of us were scared to ask any more questions, but one brave student raised his hand.

"What about Toto?"

"Of course, Toto's dead. Dogs don't live that long."

There was a shocked silence as twenty-three second graders realized their childhoods were over. I thought of my own dog, Barney. I'd assumed he'd live forever, but now that she mentioned it, he wasn't as spry as he used to be.

At recess, we stood in huddled circles discussing death, drugs, and what really happened to Mrs. Coleman's husband.

Months later, we were assigned to write a story. I wrote about two grasshoppers having a hot air balloon adventure. I thought it was good, but I wasn't sure. After Mrs. Coleman read it, she handed it back to me and said, "This is good. You have a knack for writing. Stick with it."

And I believed her. Because anyone honest enough to tell a group of second graders that Dorothy Gale died of a drug overdose isn't going to lie to spare a child's feelings.

© 2021 Sarah Belanger

April 5:
Scott Hancock

I flew Dr. von Braun to the moon. Google: 'Scott Hancock and von Braun' to find the touching story of our trip. Thanks, Alabama Space and Rocket Center.

And I enlisted in the Army, served in Vietnam with the 1st Calvary LRRP Rangers earning a Purple Heart.

Married for fifty years, I spent decades writing logistic planning documents for the Army while raising two kids. But now retired, I write for myself and for writer's groups such as the North Alabama Science Fiction and Cake Appreciation Society (NASFCAS), Huntsville Literary Association's Fiction Writers Group, and Ann C. Crispin's Dragon-Con2K Writers Group.

My Brief but Spectacular Take On...

The Proper Study of Pebbles. As a lad I collected pretty pebbles and fossils from the gravel driveway of our home. They led me into geology and paleontology which in turn led into studying history and anthropology which guided me into sociology and psychology, and of course, to touch adequately on these, well, I had to review the eight major religions of the world. In so doing I identified a number of 'golden heart threads' held in common by the eight, and drawing certain conclusions decided that instead of following one religion per se, that I should follow the guidance of those common precepts and mores most equally held by all, that these codified the best goals of mankind. But perplexingly, I seemed to be in a minority. Many people seemed to focus on what makes us different, not alike. Confounded and confused I read on many great and respected figures who over time have issued thoughts on such matters and it was in Alexander Pope's 'Essay on Man' I found much of the wisdom I sought. "Know, then, thyself, presume not God to scan; The proper study of mankind is man."

A Good Idea

A long, long time ago I served three years in the U.S. Army and I spent about the latter half of my enlistment training Rangers. This often involved taking them out 'into the field', i.e., either to the boonies up in the North Georgia woods or down to the wild swampy wetlands of Florida. Once there we would then put them through all kinds of rough situations. Little things like, all night cross-country forced marches during inclement weather, during which my fellow instructors and I would have the pleasure of ambushing them along the way of their night march. This often involved shooting off a lot of blanks and triggering multiple flash-bangs. It was a lot of fun.

But then one day my training group got a rare day off while on-site in sunny Florida, and we were told we could only simply hangout and enjoy a local 'swimming hole', one provided by the Corps of Engineers on the Federal land we were at, under the guise of flood control. Now the Corps had dredged a lot of sand out a spot along a small creek and had used the sand to build a dam just above the dredged spot, and then they laid steel drainpipes from the top of the dam to the bottom of the dredged spot to act as the dam water drains. The water traveling down the twin 40-foot-long, two-and-a-half-foot wide pipes dropped about 12-15 foot in elevation, and the current rushing out at the bottom kept the pipe exit areas downstream blasted clear of sand buildup.

There was about a five foot drop from the water surface above the dam to that of the water surface below the dam. We could swim on either side of the dam but were cautioned about the deep-water currents in the bottom of the pool downstream and that we should also be careful to not get too close to the intake ends of the pipes upstream. But did I listen? Oh no, not me.

It quickly became a game to see how close I could get to the intakes, and eventually I found myself in the water, right at the mouth of one, literally holding onto the drainpipe itself, using my hands and feet both on the pipe, fighting the current. Was I concerned? Nope. The steel corrugated drainpipe was about two and a half foot in diameter, and with my head under water I could see the sunlit bottom of the downstream pool, only 40 feet away and some quite a bit deeper. And as I stared at that light at the end of that blackened tunnel, I suddenly had this vision of me simply letting go of the pipe and allowing the current to take me down. At the rate the current was flowing I'd shoot thru the 40 feet of pipe in seconds and then I'd just swim to the surface, why, it would just be so easy! And that decided me.

So I did. And oh yes, I shot through that narrow pipe like a bullet through the barrel of a rifle and then I was out in the bottom of the pool. I wasn't quite ready for just how much the current would bang me from side to side inside the pipe during that quick trip, nor was I ready for the current to drive me face first into the roiling sand at the bottom once it ejected me from the pipe, but I quickly re-oriented myself as to which way was up and mentally cursing the fact that my eyes were now filled with sand, I quickly rose to the surface and began climbing ashore.

Breaking the surface I found many of my fellow soldiers were going a bit nuts. There was a lot of hollering going on, stuff like "He got sucked into the pipe! He's GONE! GONE!" and various other folks were running towards me as I stepped ashore and when I turned to greet them and tell them everything was fine, everyone froze in place like I had stopped time, but only for a moment, then someone yelled, "BLOOD! MY GOD, LOOK AT THE BLOOD!", and they pointed in my direction.

I actually started to turn to see what it was they were pointing at behind me, but then I saw red out of the corner of my eye, and looking down first at my arms, then to my chest, my stomach and my legs, everywhere there was blood. So much blood.

And as I stood there looking down at myself, I could now see blood slowly welling up from thousands of cuts all over my body. Not one exposed inch of skin remained unbloodied, except thankfully my face. Well, it turned out I did have a number of cuts on the tip of my nose, but my face and the front of my head had been largely protected by the fact I had gone through the pipe with my hands and arms fully extended out in front of me. My elbows and shoulders took the damage my head might have otherwise gotten.

And it also turned out that not only was the inner surface of the corrugated galvanized steel pipe extremely rough, but later investigation determined that the inner exposed corrugations had long ago begun rusting through, and I had been shooting through a metal tube filled with thousands of rusty blade-like projections, which my body had banged repeatedly against them again and again, each time inflicting countless slicing wounds, some several inches long.

I ended up spending a few days in the local hospital, during which I had to endure a lot of wound cleaning, as the doctors wanted to make sure they got out all the metal and rust particles they could, and then, after I rejoined my Company, I got chewed out not just by our First Sergeant, but several higher-ranking officers as well. Even our Battalion Commander. They each asked me what the heck had motivated me to do such a stupid thing, to which I could only reply, "Well Sir, it seemed like a good idea at the time...".

Why I Wrote This

Over the years I've received many good pieces of advice on 'how to write'. I have a library of books on the topic, - though I've only but skimmed through half of them, and only paid closer attention to a handful of those. Perhaps my writing has suffered due to me failing to pay proper attention to the wisdom offered up within my collected writing books, but even so, experience has taught me that there is one old writer's homily that most always pays off, and that old piece of advice is, "Write what you know." Truth. Of all the things I have ever written, the science-fiction, the fantasy, the mysteries, the noir detective stories, my efforts at horror, none of them have gotten the reception and acclaim from my fellow writers as my stories about my own experiences, - my memoir pieces. And then several of my writing friends told me of the *Sundial Writer's Corner* and encouraged me to write and submit a piece to them. And I did, and in doing so I relived a moment in time, to share. It seemed like a good idea at the time, and so it was.

April 12:
Jackie Williams

I grew up in Sumter County, Alabama; met my husband of fifty years during our college freshman year at the University of Alabama; graduated with a Master  of Social Work in 1973. My husband, Gene, went into the Air Force, and we spent 24 years, mostly in the Midwest (North Dakota, Nebraska). We had two sons who taught us almost enough about parenting to now be good parents. No grandchildren, yet. I had a clinical practice in Huntsville for fifteen years, where I learned more than college taught me. Now I tell stories.

My Brief but Spectacular Take On...

Higher Mathematics. I used to tease my sons (both engineers) by saying that I don't believe in Calculus: that it is just a fable made up by teachers to frighten little children. Of course, I do accept that it is real and that it possibly has a purpose. And I thank God for those who can grasp its meaning, especially in Huntsville where we send people into space. (And if not calculus, then some other kind of frightening math.) For me, it is relegated to the kind of place in my mind where I keep knowledge of other incomprehensible things like gamma rays and gravity.

It is good to accept the possible existence of things that one cannot quite grasp. Because in that world, there *might* be mermaids and unicorns.

When We Used Typewriters

One day toward the end of the last century, when my sons were in high school, I asked if they were interested in learning to type. They informed me that they were already learning to keyboard. On a keyboard, naturally. In the 1960's, we took typing, and we used typewriters.

Our typing teacher, Ms. Bea, was much like her name implies: small, full of energy, and with a rapid, clipped voice that made it seem as if she were buzzing around. The only thing I knew in advance about Ms. Bea was that once, according to my sister, she spent a whole class period wearing a slice of dill pickle on one of the lenses of her glasses, which hung from a chain around her neck.

But Ms. Bea turned out to be a dynamic teacher. She taught us typing, but also to take pride in our typing. No strikeovers under any circumstances. Keep a steady rhythm, not jump starting and then slowing down. Speed was good, but accuracy was better. Three mistakes cost ten points. Strikeovers lost you the whole paper.

We learned the proper form for a business letter, how to fold a letter correctly, how to estimate the room we would need at the bottom of a page for footnotes, and how to make a carbon copy without getting the copy on the back of the original (barely catch two pieces of paper in the machine and put the carbon paper between them with the side that would smut your nose if you got close enough toward you).

Maybe much of that is obsolete in the days of computer programs that do it all, but she also gave us the benefit of her particular wisdom, usually when she was upset about something or at someone. Sometimes we knew exactly who or what had upset her, but not always. One day, she said she wanted to talk to the boys. The girls could listen, but she wanted the attention of the boys especially. She told them that most of them, within a few years, would probably be drafted. She went on to say that they needed to learn to type, because if the Army learned they could type a little, they might be put at a desk job where it was safer. Reading the newspaper accounts of the war going on in Vietnam told us that Ms. Bea was indeed upset, but not at the boys in her classes.

We learned from her that if it is difficult to learn a task, we will be able to teach it much better. It turned out that typing was difficult for her to learn, and because it was, she had more patience teaching it, but shorthand. . . well those little squiggles made sense to her the very first time she saw them, and therefore shorthand was hard for her to teach. Her shorthand students claimed that she taught that class well too, but I had seen those squiggles and never attempted the class.

She allowed us to swap back and forth every few weeks from manual to electric typewriters. However, for me, after one of the three-week periods on an electric typewriter, she labeled me an electric cripple and, for my own good, would not let me leave the manual side of the classroom again. She also gave me some personal advice. She leaned in close to me with voice lowered, smelling of coffee, as usual, and said, "You'd better go to college and learn to do something because you will never make a living typing."

One day she told us all to stand up. We shuffled to our feet. She continued, "Put your hands on your hips. Now look at your elbows. Your rights end at your elbow. Someone else's rights begin where your elbows end."

Whether you are typing or keyboarding, Ms. Bea's wisdom is timeless, and there is only one reply: Yes ma'am, Ms. Bea. Yes, ma'am.

Why I Wrote This

My high school experience compared to that of our sons seems as different as a horse drawn carriage and a sports car. Typing was a must-have skill for many of our generation. As Ms. Bea told us, if we could type, we could earn extra money typing papers for other students. I never did that, because getting the footnotes right was a royal pain. Our children could not imagine a world where the computer didn't do most of the drudge work of getting a paper into print. However, the eternal story is the value of a good teacher. Some things remain the same. Each of our sons had teachers who taught more than the subject, and I am grateful to them, as I am to Ms. Bea and others, including my parents, both teachers.

April 19:
Beth Thames

I started writing stories almost as soon as I learned to read, but I never thought of myself as a writer until I took creative writing classes at the University of Ala-

bama. One of my professors told me I just might have some skill, but I needed to work on my craft. Fifty years later, I'm still doing that.

I've been lucky. I married the right person—my high school and college sweetheart—and we've been lucky to have two children and now two grandchildren. Our house is full of books and papers. (Note to reader: If you love to read and write, marry an English major.)

I've been lucky in my career, too. Working first as a clinical social worker and then as a college English Instructor, I began writing commentaries and essays for NPR's *All Things Considered.* This led to publication in *The New York Times*, *Atlanta Magazine*, *Southern Liv-*

ing, Working Mother, and other publications. Eventually, my hometown paper, *The Huntsville Times,* hired me to write a weekly column and WLRH aired my pieces. Thanks to Judy Watters who "discovered me" and taped my stories for *All Things Considered.*

One of the highlights of my writing career was when a D.C. cabdriver and NPR fan recognized my voice from a story I'd done about owning pets. He called me "the Alabama Cat Lady" and reduced my fare.

My Brief but Spectacular Take On...

Luck. Chance. Kismet. Fate. Whatever we want to call it, it's usually a good thing. When my family moved back to our hometown in Alabama after living in Chile' for a few years, I noticed a tall, thin boy who always had his head in a book.

He stood two rows behind me on the school steps when we had our first grade picture made. I don't remember much else about him. At recess, the boys and girls hung out in different clusters unless the teacher made us play together. We rarely did. We didn't like the same games.

My family moved again at the end of the year, this time to Maryland and Ohio. By the time I came back five years later, the boy was even taller. We talked a bit. We ran around in the same crowd at school. During the awkward dating time of the early teen years, we glanced over at each other on the dance floor, both doing The Twist with other people. His girlfriend. My boyfriend.

By the time we were 17, free from other relationships, we talked more and more. Our first date was dinner and one long conversation. After graduation, we went to different colleges, but when he transferred to mine, the conversation started again. We talked about books, politics, music, classes.

Women students had strict curfews, so when I went into the dorm to meet mine, we shifted our conversation to the telephone. We talked deep into the night. Eventually, there were just two words: "I do."

Our conversation has continued for more than fifty years. Was it luck? Was it fate? Whatever it was, it's led to gratitude. If you look across the proverbial crowded room and see the one you'd choose again, there is no way not to feel grateful.

Once people embrace gratitude, it's hard to shake it off. At a certain age, we know we're lucky to simply be here, sharing a bottle of wine with an old friend and talking. Still talking.

My Zoom Romance

When I was a child, my big sister told me the people on the television screen could see me, just the way I saw them. She was older and wiser and I believed her.

So I dressed up, brushed my hair, and sat on the couch in our den, smoothing my skirt and making sure my pony tail was neat and tied back properly. Then I stared at the screen.

I didn't know I'd be doing the same thing sixty years later. These days, I'm not staring at the Walt Disney characters on TV, but at the faces on the computer screen. Sometimes there are six. Sometimes there are sixty. They're little faces in squares. Zoom faces.

Oh, Zoom. We don't love you, but we still need you. Back when we thought you were just a summer romance, with your little boxes on the screen and the glimpses of strangers' bookcases and paintings hanging on their wall, we found you charming.

It was like going to a party again, only at home in our gym garb. We couldn't go out, so we stayed in, with you for company. You connected us to friends, near and far, and family members, young and old. We learned your odd rules about muting ourselves on screen and turning the black square with our name on it into a tv screen, where we watched ourselves talk to others on the call and wondered if we really look like that. Shouldn't we have done something more with our hair? Our makeup?

So we put lipstick on to meet with you, and checked ourselves out, the way you do when you have a new suitor. We knew we could wear pajama bottoms as long as we looked nice from the waist up, but that seemed rude, so we switched our flannel pants for dressy ones.

We got used to your freezing up every now and then, since we knew you'd come right back on your screen and talk some more. We got used to your delays, your silences, and your quirks, like asking us to enter a meeting ID number when we forgot to write it down.

We got used to the camera suddenly being on us. But wait, did someone ask a question? Are we supposed to answer? Is it our turn? What about the little chat box at the bottom of your screen—our screen? Do we chat to that or write a secret message?

Do we spy an old sweater thrown over a chair in our Zoom room? Did anyone else see it? Have we been exposed as a sloppy Zoomer, one who can't be bothered to make her office look like a room in *House and Garden* magazine? Why didn't we place flowers on the table, like other Zoomers do?

Like all summer romances, this one will eventually come to an end. We thought you'd be gone by Christmas, but here we are, Zooming along, staying at home with you, the boyfriend who won't leave.

In the far distant future, when this virus is gone and we're free to go out again, we'll look back on our relationship with nostalgia. You helped us get through a really rough time. We appreciate it. But if you're still here this summer, we'll have a talk. Maybe you'll be tired of us. We'll certainly be tired of you.

Still, we thank you for the Zoom romance. It was nice while it lasted, but it's way past time to break up.

Why I Wrote This

I like people. I especially like actual people who sit in my living room and talk to me or meet me for coffee somewhere. The pandemic allowed us to be with friends as long as they were behind computer screens and in little Zoom boxes in their own homes and offices. While I appreciate the technology behind all this and understand the need to stay safe, I've been lonely. I suspect most of us have been. After many months of staying at home and Zooming, I remembered an old boyfriend who kept calling and wouldn't take a hint. Time to say goodbye. Get out of here, please. It's over. It's so over. And that's how I feel about you, Zoom.

April 26:
Andrew V. Gonzales

Hello! My name is Andrew V Gonzales and I currently (as of writing this biography) live, work, and play in Huntsville, AL. I earn a roof over my head as

an analyst by day and stave off the specter of middle age by night. Pizza, public radio, and local markets are my love language. Co-existing with our planet is my life and I have weathered grocery totes, boxes of glass bottles, a compost bin, and solar panels to prove it. When I'm not indulging or saving the world, I am documenting my life, writing, or (my newest love) reading.

My Brief but Spectacular Take On...

Words. I love words. They are the basic unit of change. Whenever I retrieve my pocket dictionary and thesaurus from my nightstand, my wrist tingles with excitement and my heart swoons over the bound infinity. Their combinations and permutations rival the night sky. It is illegal. Unfair. How can I wield such density with so little effort? They're more like a black hole and equally destructive when wielded with little to no regard for their consequences. They, however, know no sides. They simply are. Thus, I choose to use them for good. I choose to treat them with the utmost dignity and respect for the ripples they send out into the universe will reach far beyond my own imagination. I will always feel this way about words. I will always feel the same awe and wonder staring at a blank page as I do staring up at the stars. There is so much out there and I am so small.

Sunday School #77

Many journals ago, I promised myself to visit the beach at least once per year for the remainder of my life.

As of this post, I have yet to break that promise.

It is a pilgrimage I look forward to honoring every trip around the Sun.

This trip has been exceptional. A crowded beach was no place to be in the midst of a pandemic. And hotels did not offer the level of isolation I desired. I wanted private. I wanted away.

I wanted a rental on the Gulf shoulder-to-shoulder with a national park.

By the time I found one, however, it was well spoken for. I found myself dangerously close to making this exceptional year an exception to my rule. Worst case, I would have driven to the Gulf and back in one day just to fulfill my promise (and minimize contact with people). Thankfully, it did not come to that. I was able to book my paradise at the expense of two months 'worth of waiting.

It was an exercise in patience. It paid off, in more ways than one, last week.

"I discovered a meteor shower out of Leo was peaking that very evening. It was the push I needed to stargaze for the evening. I packed what I needed and took to the darkness."
— Broadcast 16:17

I lucked out with a New Moon upon arrival.

"It was quite dark. I could, however, still make out the beach, my feet, and cresting waves. I carried a little fear throughout the evening. Every figure was a killer on the loose and every new sound was that same killer on approach. I found an isolated spot, wrapped myself up, and looked skyward with my ears trained on my surroundings. It was easy to be carried away by the night sky. So many stars. The sky was unfiltered. Each star twinkled like a candle in the distance. Under binoculars, one star turned into twenty. It was incredible to see all the forms and clusters across the sky. I could barely make out the Milky Way. In Orion, one set of clusters had a very visible blue haze much like the tail of a comet. It was so intriguing."
— Broadcast 16:18

I find it ironic that after months of waiting for and hours of traveling to the beach, I found myself, once again, traveling minutes to and waiting hours for the midnight sky to open up. It was another exercise in patience. Anything else was unwelcome.

"There is something special about patience. There is something holy about pilgrimage; when you must show up for it rather than it for you. This meteor shower wasn't on-demand. It couldn't be packed up and shipped overnight. It

was not available to stream. It wanted one thing only; patience."
— Broadcast 16:20

I watched eight-to-ten meteors over the course of that evening. Two were exceptionally brilliant. It may have taken three hours of waiting, but in those three hours, I was graced with the light of every star, crash of every wave, and caress of every grain of sand.

I shudder to think what a world without waiting looks, sounds, and feels like.

How do you spend your waiting hours?

Here's to filling each one with the world around us.

Why I Wrote This

This essay is the seventy-seventh instantiation of a writing series I called, "Sunday School". Every Sunday, for two years straight, I would read back at a week's worth of journal entries, find the verse (or verses) that spoke most to me, and write about it (or them) on my blog. Each essay included the inspiring verse(s) such that it read seamlessly. Sunday School #77 was inspired by my annual pilgrimage to the beach and the amount of patience I had to muster for it and one of its star-studded evenings.

May 3:
Cindy Small

Cindy Small, a New Orleans, Louisiana native, suddenly blew into N. Alabama following Katrina. She was born into a Jewish Viennese family who relocated

to The Big Easy from Vienna, Austria. What is so delicious about her Viennese family was that their snobbery and superiority were outmatched only by their neuroses. She had the ability to laugh at the train wreck of her life and arrive all the way to sanity.

Cindy graduated from Tulane University with an undergraduate degree in Journalism and Masters in Historic Preservation Studies.

My Brief but Spectacular Take On...

Cindy Small is a good example of surviving family dysfunction by committing to therapy and learning the enjoyment that life can bring.

Lucky to have experienced the best years that New Orleans had to offer in the 60's, coupled with mentally ill family dynamics, gave her creativity and a palate for the bohemian way of life. She survived childhood and adulthood by the ability to laugh at the train wreck of her life. It's a message to those coming from dysfunctional families that inner peace can arrive and to get there, you must laugh all the way to sanity.

What is so delicious about her Viennese family was their snobbery and superiority outmatched only their neuroses. They were consumed by their own dysfunctional minds. Her family was privileged due to better pastry and prettier music.

New Orleans: Cajun music. Creole food. Mardi Gras. Lowest public education quality in the United States. Incomprehensibly corrupt politics. A place where life is slow. Pretty. Elegant. Decadent. Sleazy.

And so her journey begins.

The Universe Waits for Me: Family Motto

During her late-life years, my mother's health began deteriorating as she complained it was just plain difficult finding a sequined colostomy bag. Lil and her best friend of 53 years, Edna, both had their colons removed at the same time, same date and at the same hospital. Years of cream-filled éclairs, copious amounts of alcohol and more cans of Vienna Sausages than the law allowed, had an effect on a human's digestive system. But Mother believed that regardless of life's obstacles, glamour was first.

Edna passed on to her sweet rewards while Mother insisted on a funeral where indulgence was required. Both had been glamorous women and also co-captains in a Mardi Gras carnival organization, thus Mother insisted that Edna look more fabulous dead than alive.

While planning the funeral, Mother was very concerned that visitors paying last respects to Edna at the church might be "fashionably challenged." God knows that would never be allowed for dear Edna. Printed invitations with Edna's vital statistics, photograph, biography and what to wear at the funeral and grave site were sent to each guest. This just wasn't any type of fashion-based funeral; this was Edna's farewell. Mother didn't believe in funeral traditions. Finally, a House of God would morph into a fabulous soiree with Edna appearing as the deceased queen.

The architecture of the church was dazzling in uptown New Orleans. The old church was built in the

Italianate style with bricks and limestone. Inside were high alters and magnificent marble crucifixes. Countless pews were draped in lavender gauze. In-between gauze was pink lace left over from my grandmother's pornographic lingerie shop along with tiny paper roses. Edna would have had it no other way. Very tastefully, mother set up a full-booze bar discreetly in a corner niche of the church while exotic incense whiffed throughout the air. Pallbearers were employees of my grandmother's lingerie store. All wore white tuxedos with purple cummerbunds and matching purple top hats. They loved Edna and they loved to party.

Edna had a history of entertaining priests in her home. The monastery was conveniently located a block away from Edna's house, and so her home was the gay hideaway for the neighborhood priests. I remember when I was a child one evening walking into her home to have dinner. Monsieur Franco was wearing a long strand of pink Marabou around his neck. He and Father Simion were rehearsing the tango, and dancing cheek-to-cheek. Mother knew that many of these priests had lived vicariously through Edna's sequined gowns. So Mother knew that inviting priests to attend Edna's funeral would be fantastic!

Directly in center-front of the church, Edna lay in state. Her emerald-green sequined ball gown overflowed outside the casket, lightly dusting the floor. She wore a giant headpiece from a prior Mardi Gras ball and mother special ordered an extra-long casket, accordingly. High above, inside the church balcony stood Edna's husband, Conrad, an opera singer. He bellowed a Viennese love song while the church choir sang and played superbly. Certainly, some guests were in an uproar over *The Patron Saint of Sequins*, my mother, Lil. This was New Orleans choreography at its finest: My mother mixed grief and celebration, making this funeral one profound party. After all, it was her responsibility to keep Edna's memory alive. Mother demanded a wild, show-biz affair with lights, cameras and action!

Heat was sweltering inside the church. Once the priest finished, church doors flung open and boys in lavender cummerbunds heaved the casket outside. A swatch of the green sequined ball gown peeked outside the casket fluttering in the summer air. The casket was positioned on a horse-drawn carriage decorated in plastic pink roses and purple bows. Crowds of friends and a jazz band led the way toward the grave site. My mother stood like a rooster behind the Holy Name of Jesus Christ priests making certain this soiree was played out perfectly. Prayers completed, Mother placed a sequined scepter on top of the casket. Pallbearers lifted the casket, pushing it inside the hole in the ground. "Oy, My God," my very Jewish mother yelled. "The casket not fit in the hole!!!" In retrospect, how could it fit, for God's sake?!? The casket was unusually long and custom made for a headpiece and ball gown. Not common fare in the funeral industry.

Mother snapped her fingers towards the grave diggers. "Hey you mens, get this hole dug immediately. Edna has to be in the ground quick. Vhat the hell's the matter with you peoples?" The diggers madly began shoveling dirt while widening the hole. I wished at that exact moment in time that I could pour a martini for Edna while she waited to relocate into her new home. She would have smiled at me with those huge red, pouty lips and winked, "Yes, sweetie, take your time. And heavy on the Vermouth."

Why I Wrote This

Since Hurricane Katrina, Cindy relocated from New Orleans to N. Alabama and decided that instead of pursuing a PhD, creating short stories was far more critical. A strange strain of cultures invaded her childhood in New Orleans, Louisiana as she quickly graduated into adulthood at a very early age. French Quarter drag queens became her best friends as her childhood centered on platinum bouffant wigs, spirit gum, sequins, eyebrow wax and lots of marabou. Preferably turquoise.

She wrote her vignettes to describe the quirkiness of her home town, New Orleans.

Cindy graduated from Tulane University in New Orleans with an undergraduate degree in Journalism and Masters in Historic Preservation Studies. There was no Drag Queen 101 course being offered at the time.

Cindy's stories are unquestionably unique, candid and totally authentic non-fiction memoirs about her family's relationships between lovers, friends, ex-friends, strangers, and just about anyone their bizarre behavior affected. The memoirs are a field guide for the aficionado of a particularly rare breed of bird, daughters of Viennese Holocaust survivors living their own kind of life in the heart of New Orleans for almost 50 years. Bizarre, and daily, family eccentricities provided her a lifetime wealth of black humor.

May 10:
Michael Guillebeau

My family moved to Huntsville in 1956, when I was 5 years old, and Huntsville, like me, was far younger than it is now. I grew up here, brought a beautiful

New York girl back home, and, with her, raised two beautiful children here.

I worked for many years as a software engineer for NASA and the DoD (what could be more Huntsville?) In 2013, I retired to write fiction full-time. Since then, I have published seven novels and over forty stories. If you've got something you've always dreamed of doing, I am the poster child of why you should get busy with it now. The grass really is greener in the land of your dreams.

My Brief but Spectacular Take On...

Growing up and growing backward. Like most people, I spent most of my life as an adult: ambitious, mature, strong. Now that my children have found their own adulthood, and my time has become my own, I've worked on shedding that tough adult skin, and growing back into a little boy: open, vulnerable, wide-eyed and often needy. I recommend it to anyone.

Poems About Mothers and Sons

Moon Tails

Scientists tell us now
that our moon has a tail.
Moon-white particles of her heart
ripped from her
by the searing light
of her partner the sun.
Her shattered bits find each other
in the emptiness of space
and join together
into an essential tail
trailing a hundred thousand miles
behind her until
they rain down on me, into me,
and become a part of me.

We are star stuff,
it is true,
and wondrous for it.
But, no less,
I absorb and become
your soft white moon tail,
my body growing
from yours
until I don't know
where your moon dust ends
where I begin.

Perhaps that is why
whenever I feel joy or love or pride,
my sun-browned face
splits open
and a toothy white line reveals
the gentle moon-tail white
built in me
by you.

A Wedding in Cana

There was a wedding in Cana, and the mother of Jesus was there... And when the wine gave out the mother of Jesus said to Him, "They have no wine." - John 2:1-3 New American Standard

Thirty-three years after
my miracle of his birth
we see his big debut:
turning water into wine,
like any bartender.
My son's holy miracle?
Catering.

This parlor trick is the sum total of my
thirty-three years of hiding
secrets and miracles in my heart.
thirty-three years of a mother's
essential nudges.

Giving any explanation but the real one.
The dirty-faced child
with the something-hidden smile,
women clucking clichés
"Isn't he special?"
I'd match his smile, say just:
"Yes, he is"
and they'd never know
the revelation they'd heard
from me.

After all the ordinary years
fussing at Joseph for wasting
my holy son's time with carpentry.
But the two of them loved
making something beautiful from ordinary wood
so my silence stretched on for years

After the whispers
When will he grow up?
Move out of the house,
make something of
his life – like the others.
I'd try to match his smile
and not say
things that couldn't be believed.
Remember: Rocks in the desert
have waited ten thousand years
for him.
It will happen
in his time.

And now his time has come.
Finally.
And they're amazed
at a cheap parlor trick
and I, like any mother,
think, "Can't he do more
with his talent?"

I look across the room,

catch his eye.
A flickering little boy smile.
This wine is sweeter
for the aging.

Why I Wrote This

As a man, I've always been fascinated by the relationship of mothers and sons. We boys grow up in the shadows of our fathers: imitating them, rebelling against them, seeing them when we look in the mirror to find out who we are. But it is our mothers who literally create us, and build the hearts that will drive us through our lives, and shine through our every action.

I am also fascinated by the fact that, even after sons grow to the point where they tower over their mothers physically and perhaps even in their achievements, there is a part of every mother who knows that their son will always be their little boy, in need of and subject to their guidance.

© 2021 Michael Guillebeau

May 17:
Monita Soni

With one foot in Huntsville, the other in India and a heart steeped in humanity, writing is a contemplative practice. Borrowing a tweet from a red cardinal, the

 wind whistling through green meadows, a child's laughter, a twinkle from fireflies, I weave poems. Nature has given me an outline of my own masterpiece. I delight in writing and coloring on my notepad. I write, rewrite and write some more. The more I write, the more I fall in love with the craft.

The stories I hear, read and recount embody me...Like old friends, bedazzled with the blessings.

My Brief but Spectacular Take On...

Pioneers. Very few women of my mother's generation painted. Miniature art flourished in the Mughal era, but artists commissioned to paint Royalty. In British India, intellectuals like Jyotindranath Tagore and Rabindranath Tagore started painting common people of India. Their art had a distinct, native, raw quality. Another renowned artist from India was António Xavier Trindade, born in Sanguem, Goa in 1870 to catholic parents. Trindade enrolled at the Sir Jamsetjee Jeejeebhoy School of Art in Bombay, a prestigious institution dedicated to the teaching of painting, sculpture and design. Trindade's work is recognized for a distinct fusion of Indian and Western Cultures. Amrita Sher-Gil was the only woman artist of that era. A Hungarian-Indian painter was "one of the greatest avant-garde women artists of the early 20th century." Her art was influenced by European masters but she found herself when she started painting in the style of Bengali Renaissance. My mother was a pioneer in her own right. Her interest in art and painting spanned her lifetime. Her home was studded with lovely pieces of art. She inspired her children, and grandchildren to paint. What a gift!

My Mother Shines Through Her Paintings

The most valuable painting in my art collection is one of my mother's masterpieces. My mother Kaushal Kapur was born in Sikar district of Rajasthan, the city studded with large airy havelis with whitewashed walls decorated with colorful Rajasthani folk murals. These Rajasthani paintings are inspired by Mughal art. Rajputana culture is exhibited in profiles of handsome Rajput men with their handlebar moustaches and elaborate turbans. Horses, camels and elephants. Beautiful maidens on rolling green hills, ebullient water springs and limpid lakes dotted with lotus blossoms. Cavorting with deer, parrots, and peacocks. One is transported to the Thar desert to a utopian Shangri La. My mother loved decorating her parents' courtyard with colorful rangolis or painting henna tattoos on friends and sisters' palms. Once at the School of Art in Jaipur, she saw an artist engrossed in painting a miniature. Miniature art was introduced to India in the sixteenth century by the Mughal ruler, Humayun. He brought with him Persian artists who specialized in the fine art of painting. The word miniature comes from 'minium' which is red lead paint used in illuminated manuscripts. These paintings are very intricate and rendered in minute detail, on paper, ivory, wood, leather, marble, and cloth. Colored with vegetable and mineral dyes in complementary colors. Pale greens, reds, blues and yellows. Embellished with real silver and gold they sparkle like multifaceted gemstones. Fine brushes were made from the hair of squirrels, and were highly valued. Today many artists replicate the originals in poster colors for affordable merchandising.

Humayun's descendent Emperor Akbar built an art gallery and many schools of painting like Mewar (Udaipur), Bundi, Marwar, Jaipur, and Kishangarh flourished in his reign. Akbar era paintings were aristocratic, and strong in portraiture. Elaborate court scenes and hunting expeditions were favored. In the eighteenth century a Rajput king Samant Singh fell in love with a poet and singer, Bani Thani. He abdicated his throne and settled in Brindavan with her. He commissioned his court painter Nihal Chand to do several paintings to document his affair de coeur. These unusually large (about 19 by 14) paintings are the finest of all Rajasthani miniatures. My mother was mesmerized by the king in light blue skin as Krishna with his beloved as Radha. She requested the master to teach her how to paint. The art teacher was reluctant, thinking that it was a passing fancy for her. He tried to dissuade her. But pursuit of creativity takes courage and persistence. Mother's resolve was apparent at a tender age. One day, the teacher asked her to draw straight lines on a blank paper. Before he could say *Radhe Krishna*, little Kaushalya had drawn a hundred straight lines on the paper. Impressed by her steady hand, the artist enrolled her in his class.

Mother painted several gouache watercolors. I grew up with her paintings in our home. They are exceptional works of art in delicate harmonious colors.

I adored her paintings as a child but over time my appreciation has increased. There is unique clarity of form and an apparent ease of composition. My eyes linger for hours on fine uninterrupted lines, and exaggerated features in the frames. Long necks, large almond eyes, delicate fingers and elegant toes. They remind me of Raphael. My mother's art is imprinted on my mind. Perhaps that explains elaborate doodles in my workbooks. My classmates would line up at my desk to request their doodles. School chalkboards were also covered in my art. My teachers can vouch for that. After coming to America, my mother visited me and we both made a Bani Thani style painting together. I can visualize her able hands patiently mixing the watercolors for me. This painting is my anchor. It portrays the universal twin souls *Radha-Krishna* engrossed in mutual adoration. I have the painting on my mantle. In the grandeur of this rendering, I can visualize my mother's being in the Bani Thani. I also have her painting of Ahalya, the most beautiful woman petrified in stone kneeling in front of a handsome Lord Rama. I have another one of a lovely young maiden on a tuft of lotus leaves with a serene expression which I think is a self-portrait.

I never feel alone when I paint because my mother's hand guides me from across the oceans. I have painted a portrait of Bani Thani in a gold stamped veil for my mother and she loves it. But my piece de resistance is her prize-winning painting of a maiden in a hut waiting for her beloved. It is a 9 by 11 monochromatic watercolor painting in shades of green and aqua. She has created a wonderful rustic atmosphere and depth with a limited palette. Color blending is flawless. I can enter the living space, hear the rustle of her skirt. Touch her long fingers, admire her delicate lashes as she engages in small talk with her parrot. As a child I often wondered what she was cooking on the earthenware stove. The solitary lamp in the alcove and four flickering flames are so poetic. But more than anything else, I love her beautiful feet strongly planted on terra firma despite the faraway look in her eyes. The painting embodies the body, heart and soul of my mother. She is an angel and the salt of the Earth. And... she is mine.

Why I Wrote This

Appreciation of the visual arts was encouraged by my mother in early childhood. Our hobby satchel had a sketch pad and color pencils and a slender box of *Camlin* watercolor cakes. Mother encouraged us to observe Nature and reproduce the likeness on paper. She would hold it at an arm's length and render positive appreciation. She had a fine eye. Her gouache paintings are remarkable. I cannot even try to emulate her fine work rendered with a "mouse-whisker" brush! When I came to the US, I immersed myself in European masters. Monet, Manet, Picasso, Pissaro, Rembrandt and Vangogh. I did several paintings myself borrowing from the impressionists, surrealists and the cubists. I brought my colorful, many -layered paintings and collages back home to Bombay as gifts for my parents. They received them with great alacrity. During the pandemic, I could not travel to India. I was worried about my mother. To soothe my nerves, I painted on every surface I could lay my hands on. Canvas, fabric, paper, parchment, glass, ceramic, stones. The process of drawing, stippling, spinning the color wheel and painting brought me to my mother's side. I could feel her hand and eyes upon me as I painted. I could be with my sweet mother through the magic portal of her Bani-Thani paintings.

May 24:
Chris Ferguson

My name is Chris Ferguson and I am a writer of poems and short stories. As a member of the Huntsville Literary Association poetry group, I look for inspiration by considering alternative viewpoints about ideas related to our collective human experience. Writing short stories for the *Sundial Writers Corner* offers another opportunity to put into words my notions of what I believe may not be obvious. Influenced by a family history of aviation, flying has captured my imagination since I was a boy. My curiosity often leads me down small paths to serendipity and epiphany.

My Brief but Spectacular Take On...

It is the chase that grabs attention. Just like a lion that sees sudden movement and jumps up to go after whatever it was that ran past without explanation. A pursuit results and sometimes a juicy meal is the result. Life throws that type of movement at us constantly. The older we are, the less attention we give to the movements we have seen many times before. The younger we are, the more we pursue them. What never changes is the value of the chase. Young or old, what we pursue is what we value the most and that changes significantly as we experience more life. Some chase the same thing for a whole lifetime, but never catch it and have difficulty finishing the pursuit. This often leads to a repeated pursuit of the same thing in the future. Without catching what got attention to begin with, questions remain unanswered.

Hope, fear, greed, curiosity, war, peace, hunger and love form the questions we pursue. Chasing answers to our dreams and nightmares is what drives us and ultimately makes us who we become.

Art is a pursuit of questions and like the lion, all are born with the need for answers. Of course, not all questions are worthy of a pursuit, but answers always form the art of our pursuits and in turn, ourselves.

My Human Evolution

On April 12, 1961, Yuri Gagarin was the first human to leave planet Earth for the abyss of outer space. He traveled at 17,500 mph and orbited the earth once, then descended back to the planet's surface in his flaming spacecraft before ejecting and floating to the surface with a parachute. For his journey, he took an important companion. It was human nature. Together they traveled away from the place where it was created, developed and existed for millennia. That moment resonates with me. It was a bold, unbelievably audacious attempt to deliberately evolve our collective human nature, willfully imagining a future that nature itself could not.

I want to evolve. It has been a lofty ambition of mine since I was a child. I watched *Superman* on TV when I was a boy, always thinking of how I could simply jump up and start flying over the countryside. Lifting cars up with one arm, no problem, I could do that, too. In a way, the very idea of superman was a wish by Joseph Shuster and Jerry Siegal to evolve our collective human nature into something that nature could not. But here was Yuri in 1961, chasing that wish and making it come true.

Older now, I realize the significance of that realization and how it evolved not just myself, but all of us. Terrestrially territorial and competitive to our own detriment. But through our own willful, deliberate choice, we are now extra-terrestrial. With this comes much more possibility and responsibility. Knowing we are but one species from the planet Earth reveals a path to evolve that nature did not provide. "Hello, my friend from Alpha Centauri, how are you? And your family? We, the humans of Earth would like to offer you gifts of our appreciation to demonstrate our compassion and friendship." The evolution of our species will require us to see each and every one us as humans from earth. Human nature will then meet the nature of Einstein's space and time and its inhabitants, which, most likely will be very different from us. Our newly evolved views could give ideas to thrive. Humans will evolve from the nature of outer space, other planets and of course other species and I welcome the idea that my descendants will evolve beyond the human nature that sometimes drives me to consider how white my teeth are, if my hair looks good, or if my car is clean. Imagining a time and place so long from now, where appreciation of human life for its biologic complexities which cause emotion, curiosity, and uniqueness, and where I could actually jump into the air and fly over the mountain in a single bound is what I want to evolve to.

In just a few years, humans will walk on Mars. After all that has been shouted from mountaintops, scratched on stone, etched in clay, painted on papyrus, printed in a book or viewed on a screen, this one event will move human nature beyond what living on earth for millennia has taught us. We will evolve and I am ready.

It will be written.

Why I Wrote This

Deliberately choosing to define my own identity has been a lifelong challenge. Identity informs all of my relationships. How I, with others, choose to engage in situations always affects the outcome, and my desire is to strive for a positive outcome for all involved, by offering an honest, thoughtful, and deliberate identity of myself. I try to provide something others find useful for contributing their best to a mutual situation.

The dawn of commercial space travel inspired me to consider identity. Realizing that my identity was a product of age-old human nature, I read of Yuri Gagarin's accomplishment and realized the significance of it as it applied to not just my own identity, but the identity of every race of human on planet Earth. We are all but one species.

May 31:
Erin Konstantinow

Erin Konstantinow grew up in southern California but is growing old in northern Alabama.

She is a lover of mercy, language, Truth, cats, coffee, her children, artichokes, and the smell of new tires. She is terrified of loss, loud noises, gorillas, and the abandoned AMC movie theater on Old Monrovia Road.

Formally trained as a visual artist, Erin taught high school in Los Angeles around the turn of the century. She left the classroom and moved to central Arkansas to raise her daughters, who have in turn grown up and taught her everything she needed to know about life and love and everything else.

Dead Rituals of Special Personhood

A stale earliness hovers over us
in our dark.
Sweet monochromatic cycles
trimmed in newsprint and rush.

You leave
a still quiet warmness;
A residue
you have left

The train is unrelenting in its patterns of
light and sound
It convulses, pulling and jerking
indecisively.

You were catastrophically failed by your bigness.
Gasping for the no air and
becoming a vapor.
Was I there, just for a second?
What was I wearing?

The private cadence of our love and hatred
now loudly labors to define itself.
Once again, I am lying. Lied to.

In truth we were a million broken pieces before the building ever fell.

Withered and languishing,

too easily we succumb to your injuries.

And I ache. Splintered.

In my room full of sticky thick longing,

I am the last one off the plane.

Why I Wrote This

In the immediate aftermath of my brother's death in the terrorist attacks of September 11, 2001, I found an immeasurable amount of solace in a small blue journal given to me by a colleague. I'd journaled all my life, but never in the wake of such a staggering personal loss.

I wrote tirelessly in an attempt to capture in words a picture of that day and all its details. I sought to preserve every one of the countless memories I could of the 31 years leading up to the moment when, in an instant, he transitioned from is/does to was/did.

This particular piece speaks to the complicated nature of the relationship he and I shared. I was a year and 16 days older than him. He was an athlete and I was an artist. Unsurprisingly, I remember our life growing up being characterized by the intense love and hatred that most siblings experience to some degree or another.

His name is Brent James Woodall. He worked on the 89th floor of the south tower as a Vice President of Equity Trading for Keefe, Bruyette, and Woods. He also played rugby, just bought a home in New Jersey, had a new puppy, and was expecting his first child in April 2002. I miss him terribly.

June 7:
Jon Macri

My family moved to Madison when I was only one
year old. I live with my two brothers, Mom, Dad, and
a big white dog named Keeva. I enjoy playing guitar

and piano. I'm always happy to be outside and I really
like hiking. I like reading A LOT. I'd like to study ro-
botics someday.

My Brief but Spectacular Take On...

Being a kid....I like it. I like that I can do the things that help me feel like myself...like running around. It just feels right and it's ok because I'm a kid. I have the time and no one needs me to do other things yet. There doesn't have to be a point. Like hiking, I don't have to get somewhere. I just like going and being outside. Everyone starts out a kid. I know I won't ALWAYS be a kid, but I'm happy to be one now. I hope that other people can be happy as who they are, even though it's always changing.

The Beast of Monte Sano

Gather 'round, I'll tell you a tale
that'll make your hair curl and your kiddies wail.
Way up high on this here mountain,
for years far more than I am countin'
a beast lurks atop Old Monte Sano.
Listen up, it's a fright and I'll explain so.
Deep in the woods where the sun can't shine,
Past the end of the trails, in the oaks and the pine,
Where the birds don't sing and the deer won't go
Lives the mysterious BobTurtle of Monte Sano.
If you hear a rustle, don't turn away,
It'll be gone in a flash, before you can say
Did you see a huge shell? Was that a furry tail?
Were those really fangs? With glowing eyes and claws like nails?
Reptilian feline, part turtle part cat
Its shell like armor and built for combat.
If you go looking, you won't likely find,
So scarce, it's rarely seen by mankind.
Hearing so keen with those big, pointy ears
and sense of smell that'll leave you in tears.
It'll smell you and run before you come near.
You'll wonder was the BobTurtle really just here.
If you do see it, don't stare, just run…
Once provoked, it's fierce. Your life could be done.
So next time you're hiking near the end of the path,
Turn around. Don't bring on the BobTurtle's wrath.
Turn around quickly when you get to the end,
Go back home and warn all your friends!

Why I Wrote This

I wrote this poem for a contest. It's about BobTurtles. During COVID, my family spent more time outdoors. We got to hike more as a family and enjoy the nature nearby. I had just seen the old Disney movie, Davy Crockett, before going on a family hike to Monte Sano. We had a great time. I decided to write a poem about it as if I were Davy Crockett, telling a tall tale.

June 7:
Bryan McNeal

My name is Bryan McNeal. After originally growing up in Florida, I moved to Huntsville right before my freshman year of high school, and that is when I be-

gan to take my writing seriously. Although I'd never taken any formal creative writing course up to this point, I decided to write as much as I could in my free time. Throughout high school, my writing improved and I won awards (Gold Medal from the Scholastic Art & Writing Awards) and participated in a creative writing course. Now, I currently attend Auburn University as an English Major with a Creative Writing Concentration.

My Brief but Spectacular Take On...

Authenticity and personhood. As an avid reader from a young age, I'd always been drawn to works with dynamic characters, people who felt astonishingly real beyond the page. Once my interests expanded to poetry when I was older, poems that felt like they had the poet's soul and truth embedded in them always stuck with me long after I'd read them. For me, writing was that gateway to my own self-expression and the stepping stones of my own individuality, and through poetry, I was able to be authentically myself. I feel that writing is a mirror that allows one to purposefully see themself reflected back and begin to assert their own self-worth independent of what roles or values society may place upon them. As an individual who is a part of two marginalized communities, it is in not only my own self-interest but that of individuals like me, that my writing is a reflection of me and gives someone else that experience I once had as a child--that what I wrote feels real and almost tangible to them.

Escapade with Poseidon

For days,
We called that house home.
Soaked bodies in salty brine
And made the sun kiss our supple skin.
These were moments where serenity
Revealed his face to me.
Moments when I couldn't distinguish
The genesis of the joy that blossomed
In the chambers and capillaries of this red fruit.
Maybe it was the way the music of the sea
Accentuated the sand between my toes,
Evoking memories of nereids and sea gods.
Maybe it was the way he glowed,
Body like a bronze Adonis,
Every little river in the world running down
His skin, water droplets fragmenting light
Into a halo around him.

I thought of him as an angel.
No, I thought of him as a god.
And if you saw him, you'd agree.
One day, we decided to dive together.
Air heavy in my chest as we swam beneath
The waves. I watched him carefully,
In awe with the way he called the water home,
The way with how he seemed to belong here,
A beauty among the fish.
I called him a mermaid, once, and he grinned

At me, saying that maybe the stories are true.
On my escapade with Poseidon, I let this god's
Name resound on the folds of my tongue.
Let this god's glory rock me like the waves
Of his crystal blue kingdom.

Why I Wrote This

This was written as a follow-up to a poem I'd written prior, titled "The Beach House." As someone who is content with my own queerness, I wanted this poem to be a representation of the development of an individual's queer identity. Often, it can be difficult for heterosexual people to fully grasp the nuances and complexities of queer attraction, but they're both quite similar. For many queer individuals, the first people we truly fall in love with are our friends, or other people we're well acquainted with. Although this poem is about a fictional event, it was inspired by a person for whom I hold a deep love. I chose Poseidon as a metaphor for emotions that can be awe-inspiring, deep and confusing, or perhaps even a little volatile--and maybe, it functions as a paragon of a person, someone who leaves a long-lasting impression on us.

June 14:
Madeline Rathz

I was born in Austin, Texas but spent most of my life in Huntsville, Alabama. Currently, I'm a UAB Blazer studying psychology and working on my third novel,

which, for once doesn't center around royalty — the princess is only a secondary character. I love spending time with my friends and family, crossing items off my to-do list, and obviously, writing. One of the biggest things I've learned so far in college is that I'm still figuring out who I am. My writing is constantly changing with me, but I will never lose my passion for creating new worlds or spending time with my characters.

My Brief but Spectacular Take On...

Cultivating my mental garden. As I have grown older, it becomes easy to get caught up in the monotony of the daily grind, while letting the fruits of my imagination wither away. Where does losing oneself with a pen and a notebook and a vision of princesses and mermaids fit into the pragmatic regimen of a college student pursuing a medical career? But if I've discovered one thing since moving on campus, it's that I can't perform my best at the necessary but mundane tasks of life when I've neglected my imagination. So even if it's just for fifteen minutes, I try to set time aside for myself daily to cultivate my mental garden, watering and growing it into a myriad of blooms, be it through reading a few pages, jotting down a new idea in my journal, or writing a chapter of my novel.

Skywatching

The sun dipped beneath the plane of the horizon, the sky awash in a gradient of gold, magenta, and navy. The higher Diana's eyes wandered, the more densely concentrated the first stars of evening became — twinkling grains of salt on a canvas of darkness. The afternoon clouds had dispersed into cotton wisps, and Archer and the twins leapt about capriciously, chanting, "The stars are coming out! The stars!"

Diana tucked her mittened hands into the folds of her coat as an icy gale whipped across the plain from the snow-capped mountains behind. Her thermos of tea had long since gone cold, and it sat at her feet, untouched with her sack-dinner. She traced a line in the tall grass with her boot sole, enjoying the crush of the velvet soft blades. Of course, they sprang back within moments. She dragged her foot across the same line, forcing them down again.

"Twins! Ryan! Come help me with this tent!" called Mama A, the affectionate name that all four of the Arnold children, even Diana, called their mother. Mama A's long, dark ponytail whipped around in its scrunchie as she turned to face the kids, and her dress — black and patterned with constellations and their corresponding names — was plastered to her legs as the wind tore through its skirts.

With a clamor of excitement, Stella, Ryan, and Archer, who was the oldest of the three at nine-years-old, bounded over to help Mama A stake tent poles in the ground. Diana sighed, plopping down on her sleeping bag, and watched them work, the kids all enthusiastic, clumsy hands as they fumbled with the poles and Mama A directing with all the zeal of a chorus leader. Even in the smallest pursuits, she was relentless.

Soon the tent transformed from a heap of green nylon to a dome resemblant of the picture on the box. The children clapped, applause for a successful performance. Mama A spread a worn blanket across the ground for the four of them to watch the stars, and Diana burrowed into her sleeping bag to ward off the brisk autumnal chill.

The sky had turned a silky midnight blue and thousands of stars shone against the celestial backdrop.

"I can see so many!" Archer exclaimed, diving onto the blanket and wrinkling Mama A's handiwork. The twins leapt after him, and they were a pile of squirming limbs in the darkness as they situated themselves for a night of stargazing.

"They're beautiful, aren't they?" Mama A mused, unruffled by the commotion and the complete disaster he and the twins had made of the blanket. "Out here there's less light pollution to obstruct our view of the night sky."

The twins' eyes darted from her to the whorls of stars across the sky, their expressions rapt. Even Diana had to admit that she'd never seen an evening like this.

"Light ploo-shion?" Stella struggled to sound out the unfamiliar word.

Mama A smiled and her eyes lit up like they always did when she got the chance to share her passions with her children. Only she could keep two rambunctious six-year-olds engaged in an astronomy lesson.

She sat down on the edge of the blanket and crossed her ankles, looking more relaxed than Diana had ever seen her. Though she always tried to maintain an optimistic façade for the children, Diana knew that working two part time jobs and raising four kids as a single mother was no easy task.

"Each year, when I was younger, my parents would take my siblings and me to this exact spot. And each year, they told us stories — about the constellations and the myths that inspired their names."

"Like Per-see-us?" Ryan sounded out, tugging at Mama A's skirt where the letters were printed in white beneath the linework image of the Greek hero.

"Yes, just like Perseus!" She laughed, and in the silence that followed, Diana could hear the echoes of her melodic voice mingle with the gentle soughing of trees and the burbling of a distant stream. She had heard these stories once when her mother had taken her here, just the two of them, before Archer was born. Still, her ears perked up despite herself, and she found herself leaning forward in her sleeping bag, drawn in by the smooth cadence of Mama A's voice.

"If you look just there—" She pointed toward a cluster of stars overhead, forming a sort of boxy shape. "That's Perseus's head. And there —" she traced her finger down an invisible line. "Is his body."

"That doesn't look like a person, Mama A," Archer said, rolling his eyes and curling up in the blanket.

She laughed again, the musical sound ringing through the clearing. "No, it doesn't quite, does it?

But try to imagine —" She raised her hands high. "A tall and mighty warrior, bearing sword and shield—"

"Was he handsome?" Stella interrupted.

"Aww Stella, that's gross!" Ryan leaned over and tried to tug her hair, but she wrestled out of his grasp and fell across Archer.

"Get off me!" he grumbled.

"Don't you want to know what happens?" Mama A teased, and with no further prompting the three younger siblings scrambled back to their original positions. When they were settled at last, she began.

Why I Wrote This

My story, "Skywatching," explores a teenage girl's special bond with her mother. I have been so lucky to have a similar bond with my own wonderful parents. My mother taught English and introduced me to writing by transcribing the stories I babbled about my toys and their adventures. My dad has always been there to lift me up when I feel low and remind me that I am enough even when I receive a rejection letter or a bad grade. "Skywatching" was inspired by some of my family experiences. Each year, we would attend Astronomy Day, an event at the planetarium on Monte Sano. I was always fascinated by the presentations about constellations and loved to learn the stories that inspired their names. During the pandemic, my parents, sister, and I set out blankets in our backyard and spent time together watching meteor showers and spotting constellations – Hercules, the Big Dipper, Orion. Those moments are special memories that I will take with me always, no matter what my future brings.

June 21:
Kathryn Tucker Windham

One of America's greatest storytellers, Kathryn Tucker Windham, began learning her craft as a child, listening to voices in her house, and as a 12-year-old

movie reviewer for *The Thomasville Times*. After graduating Huntingdon College in 1939, she became the *Alabama Journal's* first female reporter, and later became a reporter for the *Birmingham News*. In 1956, she began reporting for the *Selma Times-Journal* and won accolades for writing and photography. As a member of the Selma City School Board, she also stood against segregationists trying to block school integration, and had a garbage can thrown through her car windshield for her efforts. In the 1960s, she refocused her reporting skills on sleuthing true ghost stories from across the Deep South, and began to gain a worldwide following as an author and live storyteller. Mrs. Windham also created a long series of radio segments for NPR, Alabama Public Radio and in WLRH's Sundial Writers Corner, where we still enjoy her stories today with permission of her family. *(Mrs. Windham passed away on June 12, 2011. Her biography is shared by Brett Tannehill)*

How to Tell a Story

People ask me every now and then, "How do you know what's a good story?" Well, that's hard to answer. It's something that has to be answered with every audience and every teller. But I don't think you can tell a story unless you like that story. I like real stories about real people. And so I guess that's why I mainly tell family stories. Stories that capture our imagination and stories that make us laugh. And back in the recesses of every adult mind are the funny experiences that they've had, that they need to talk about with their family, and laugh about with their family.

We don't tell enough stories to make us laugh, and we need to laugh. Little short stories are fine. And don't mind if you have to hesitate a little bit in the story while you think about what you want to say next. I'm inclined to do that. I take a little breathing spell and think about what comes next. I had that analyzed one time by someone who told me that I had those pauses in my stories because I learned to tell stories by listening to my father. He smoked a pipe, and he would stop every once in a while during his story to light his pipe, or to knock the ashes out, so it was just natural to have a little pause in the story and it never bothered anybody. Don't worry about the pauses.

Don't memorize the story. Tell it naturally and tell it a little different each time, it doesn't matter. There may be someone in the audience who tells you 'That's not how you told it last time.' But stories grow and change with the telling. The main thing is to tell the story that you care about, and to tell it with enthusiasm. Let the audience know through your telling that this is something you think is important and you want to share it with them.

And don't go back over a story. Once you've told it, quit. I think that's one of the most important points of storytelling is to quit when you're through, and to know when you've told the story. And if you're a teacher, or anybody else I guess — but teachers are inclined to do this — don't ask 'Well, what did you get out of the story?' That just kills the story. Everybody listening should get something different out of the story. Different pictures painted in everybody's heads. Different memories stirred. Because that's what storytelling does. It stirs our memories. And it reminds us that life is important and exciting.

June 28:
Jimmy Robinson

I first experienced the satisfaction of hearing my own voice reading my poems and short prose on the *Sundial Writers Corner* with production master Judy Watters and have continued with current producer Dorrie Nutt. I've been writing since college at the University

of Alabama where I had undergraduate poetry writing classes with Thomas Rabbit and Everett Maddox. I later studied Latin American Literature at the National Autonomous University of Mexico while living in Mexico City, hometown of my wife, Guadalupe. Returning to Huntsville, I got involved with The Huntsville Literary Association's monthly poetry workshop group with whom I have met regularly for three decades now. I eventually became an assistant editor of their nationally circulated poetry magazine, *POEM*. I taught Spanish at Huntsville High and in the Department of Foreign Languages and Literatures at UAH.

Cee Gee's Convent Garden

A square of tall privet encloses the front yard,
small and meek with only enough space
for a single over-hanging dogwood with branches
shading a bird bath of concrete, mortar, and rock.
A few hollies and boxwoods huddle in the corners,
and a "Y" of short paths covered with creek bed gravel.
The front porch has been enclosed with glass
where Cee Gee sat in later years to watch birds
descend from branches to splash themselves
or peck at the seed she provided daily at its edges
across the seasonal interchange of species.

There is a bumper sticker boasting affiliation
with the "Feminist Chorus" which presents
concerts open to the public at both
the winter solstice and vernal equinox to celebrate
a life of sisterhood and solitude, singing songs
from a variety of cultures, countries, different epochs,
connecting the women of the town
from house to house, apartment, room to room,
neighborhood to other neighborhoods, city to city, region
to region, country to country, continent to continent,
with others on around the world.

The car hasn't been moved in months.
Cee Gee herself relinquished driving before the state
could take away her license. She had everything
she needed here to not only survive, but thrive
even as her walk turned feeble and memory played
its tricks as she fumbled for the names of the herbs
she seeded in the lumber-boxed garden her son
constructed inside the private fence behind the house.

There is only a little grass to mow and trim in front
beneath the hedge, sprouting through the creek stones
in the driveway, and along the flagstone walkway
between the house and elevated garden in the back
where I come every few weeks to wage persistent battle
with the poke, unrelenting kudzu, invading weeds and vines.
I listen for a moment at the back door
where she used to emerge to contribute to my devotion,
and even though I know the house is empty now,
I sometimes hear the mesmerizing mystic chant
of Hildegard von Bingen emanating from an inner room.

Why I Wrote This

I wrote "Cee Gee's Convent Garden" to pay homage to a lady for whom I cut grass at her home which I found enchanting with its lush, tightly-compacted varieties of flowering plants, herb garden, and bird bath evoking the mystical medieval German herbalist healer, composer of choral music and saint, Hildegard von Bingen. Producer Dorrie Nutt kindly corrected my pronunciation of the name during our recording session.

July 5:
Lynne Berry Vallely

I have been teaching religious works of art in a Sunday School class at the Church of the Nativity for over 20 years.

My co-teacher brings in poetry that also illuminates the subjects we have chosen. I have written for the *Sundial Writers Corner* since 2008. On great mornings, I am up by 5:30 a.m. sitting in my grandmother's rocking chair with my coffee, watching the sun come up over the neighborhood and contemplating a painting. I set myself the task of describing it which makes me focus on it. Eventually it speaks to me and makes my life richer.

My Brief but Spectacular Take On...

Creativity. My ability to write these pieces is obviously not mine alone. I believe that if you have read this far in this book and are reading these words, you too can write short essays like these and yours could be much better. What does it take? A willingness to set aside the time and to find a quiet space with minimal distractions. Are there things you know you want to say? Or can you invite the Muse to fly in and sit on your shoulder and point you in a direction, as I just did this morning?

Once you have that direction, can you dance between receptivity, wool gathering, and laser focus as you capture words and sentences with a butterfly net? I need an external prompt – a work of art – to provide my path. I envy those who don't, who have subjects in their heads and words ready to spill onto the page.

For me, this started as an exercise. I've always wanted to be a writer. I love the literal art of writing – blue fine-point rolling ball pen applied to paper, the shapes of words, how it feels to write them and see them on the page. And I always work out my thoughts with pen and paper. If something is bothering or challenging me, you can bet I'll pull out my journal or any paper I can lay my hands on and write it out.

So one day in 2007, I decided that if I really wanted to be a writer, I needed to make a start. My time was limited, so I decided that every morning before work, I would write for twenty minutes or so. But what to

write about? I had no idea, no plot floating around in my head, no topic, nothing. I sat at my desk and looked around. There was a large art book. I pulled it to me and opened it. I decided that I would try to hone my ability to describe something by describing a work of art that appealed to me. I turned pages until I came across "Russian Fair" by Boris Kustodiev. I described the scene, the people, the activity. Words spilled out, were captured, corralled, and organized. And somewhere during that process, the Muse flew in and sat on my shoulder and creativity began. That's one way to interpret it. Or I could say that the act of describing the painting gently unlocked the part of my brain where creativity resides. Whatever. All I know is, twenty minutes later I had a short essay on a painting that turned into a meaningful reflection. I had lost time, which happens when one is fully absorbed, and I was surprised by the outcome. It seemed not to be any work on my part but something that came through me – as if I got in a car and started driving and then, after a bit, let go of the wheel and found myself in a really interesting place.
Try it!

Canaletto

Canaletto painted so many scenes of Venice. They are instantly recognizable – a canal, of course, a long perspective, emphasis on the architecture, people small and insignificant. This one is called "The Molo in Front of the Doge's Palace."

I want to be there. I want to be in Venice now. I want to be one of those people dwarfed by my surroundings, strolling in the sun across a broad plaza in relaxed, quiet conversation with my husband or my best friend. We are discussing either the meal we just enjoyed or our next meal. We walk so much every day that we don't have to worry about gaining weight.

I've heard that a lot of Venice is made up of very narrow, dark passageways and that it's easy to get lost. Not in this painting. We are in front of the Doge's Palace. We have gotten our bearings. Maybe we will go back to the hotel and take a nap. Tonight we'll find an amazing restaurant. We'll sit outside and watch the gondolas gliding to and fro, listen to the soft lap of the water and the banter of the gondoliers. We will drink some local wine that gently slips right down into our bloodstream, sealing our communion with this city. With so much sensory overload, we will be only vaguely aware that the beautiful light has gradually stolen away. The moment eventually comes when we know we must pay our bill, find our legs, and make our way back to our hotel. But what was a stroll through architectural delights on the way to dinner has now become a completely unfamiliar challenge. It is well and truly dark. We have let a bit too MUCH wine slip into our system. There are shadows and there is uneven pavement, there are dark deep waters in these canals. People who looked friendly in the daytime look sinister and threatening as they hurry past. We take a wrong turn or two and realize we have come to a dead end. We are completely off the beaten path in an area where there's not even a sinister-looking person to ask for directions. We experience what some call the Black Panic of Venice.

Hopefully without arguing too much or getting mugged or falling into a canal, by trial and error we make our way out, we gradually, street by street, reconnect with the flow of humanity headed here and there, so close in these narrow lanes that we could touch them. We want to HUG them. We finally make it back to our hotel and collapse on our bed.

In the morning, we are starving. The adrenaline from last night's misadventure burned off most of the calories from dinner. It's another beautiful day. We dress and make our way to the plaza in front of the Doge's Palace where the sunlight bathes us and this glorious building in a benevolent golden glow. We stroll through slowly, stomachs rumbling with hunger, on our way to a glorious breakfast and a day spent exploring, ducking into a church or a museum or a shop but always returning to the touchstone of the light, the sun on the plaza, on the buildings, on the water.

This painting can be seen in the Gemaldegalerie in Berlin and on the Facebook page ©Art on the Radio.

Why I Wrote This

I am ambivalent about Venice. I've never been there. I have loved every place I've ever been in Italy and would happily return. But I can't seem to get myself to Venice.

When I was single, I often traveled on my own. In 2010, I signed up for a Smithsonian trip to Venice. But as the departure date approached, I found myself less and less enthusiastic. Finally I allowed circumstances at work to provide the excuse I was subconsciously looking for and I canceled.

This summer, as COVID eased, I reasoned that this was the time to visit Venice. I wanted to see it with my husband before the crowds returned. I had heard and read about the impact of cruise ships and wanted us to slip in before they did. But it was not to be. The delta variant and unrelated family health problems reared their ugly heads. We canceled.

My conception of Venice is much like one of those Carnival masks that is white and smiling on one side and black and frowning on the other. On the white smiling side we have the beautiful colors of the palazzos reflecting on the water, the unique architectural blend of Gothic, Byzantine, and Ottoman, small boats of all kinds, especially gondolas, centuries-old coffeeshops, great restaurants, and truly fine hotels with impeccable service and rooms with a view.

Yet I am strangely aware of the other side of the mask. And that is unusual for me as I am usually a happy, curious explorer. But those canals — could you easily fall in? There are water taxis that people stand in as they navigate the traffic. Not me. At night, the water, lovely with the reflection of light, is also dark and deep and right there. And is it clean? Does it smell? This entire city — it never dries out. Is there mold and mildew? The narrow, picturesque passage-ways and alleys — I've heard it's so easy to get lost. And the art. Perhaps my taste is not sophisticated enough. I can so easily immerse myself in the Renais-sance art of Florence. But the art in Venice is more vivid. Think Titian - big overblown exaggerated dra-matic works that make me feel jangly, that don't, to me have the inner peace nor the mastery of Leonardo, Michaelangelo, Botticelli.

So when I turned a page and found this Canaletto, I felt obliged to explore it. I was attracted to the peacefulness and spaciousness. I was envious of the artist who was able to see Venice at that time in its history. All I had heard and read about Venice applied itself to this scene so that as I described it, without ever having been there, I was able to inhabit it.

I hope to get to Venice one day. I'll try to find this site. If I am very fortunate, it will be a sunny day, un-crowded, and I will approach it with no preconceived notions.

© 2021 Lynne Berry Vallely

July 12:
Matthew Wilson

Well, let's see here. I was born in Corbin, KY, but when I was a wee six months old, my Dad retired  from the Army and we moved to Huntsville, where my Mom had grown up. I went to school at Jones Valley Elementary, Whitesburg Middle, and Grissom High, where I was both on the football team and in the concert band. I proceeded to college at West Point in New York and then began my time in the Army. Shortly thereafter I married the former Johanna Kirsch, also a native Huntsvillian. After six years of active duty we moved back home and are happily raising our two young daughters here.

My Brief but Spectacular Take On...

Lawns! I have one of the best lawns in town, hands down. No, I haven't won any awards for it, but it is extremely drought tolerant and army-worm resistant. Even better, it takes practically no effort at all—just mow it every now and then!

See, my yard is a veritable hodgepodge of grass (I honestly don't even know what kind), clover, dandelions, and other miscellaneous weeds. I save time in the fall because I don't have to rake up my leaves—just mow them into mulch and they decompose by spring!

Now don't get me wrong, I like a nice-looking lawn as much as the next person. It's (usually) edged, curbs are clean, it's not scalped, and so forth. I just don't put money into making it artificially look better. The way I figure, my neighbors, who see my lawn the most, know me and know that I'm a pretty good guy. So I don't have to impress them with my lawn. To anyone driving by, the brief glimpse looks as good as any other yard in the neighborhood. Win-win!

An Office With a View

I've never had an office with a window before. Okay, that's not strictly true. There were those three months where my window of the aluminum pre-fab gazed serenely upon the wall of another pre-fab about two feet away.

So.

I've never had an office with a view before. I went to the old Grissom High School, the one with the pods, musty air, and no windows. In college, the class-rooms were in the basement, probably to keep us engineers-in-training from realizing we were in the lab well past sundown. After that, various wooden shacks, the aforementioned pre-fab, and the shotgun seat of intimidating vehicles served as my offices. Those, you see, were during my stint in the Army. I suppose the vehicles had windows, but usually I was looking down at my map, or messing with the radio, or it was just plain dark outside.

So.

I've never had an office with a nice view before. After the Army, I started working on the Arsenal, where I got a very nice view of history by working in a converted rocket test control room. Rockets can be dangerous, though, so the control room had five-foot thick concrete walls, giant blast-proof doors, and no windows:

But "the only constant in life is change," so here I am now, four days out of five, looking out over my laptop into my front yard across the seasons. It didn't start this way, oh no. At first, I was sitting in a chair with my bed as a desk. Next, a folding TV-tray table served well for a while. Eventually, my wife and I cleaned up the spare room and declared it my office. More things eventually accumulated: the old desk in place of the tray, the extra monitor, the board on the wall where I hang up artwork from my kids.

It turns out I really do have a nice front yard. In the summer, lots of local kids ride their bikes down the sidewalk on their way to the neighborhood pool. I could actually watch the leaves changing color in the fall, instead of idly noticing as I walked in from the driveway. We were blessed with just a touch of snow this year and I could enjoy the sight of it falling. I could literally see the weeds growing in the spring, and all those thunderstorms were fun to watch rolling in.

I know this won't last forever. Eventually the desk will go back to the garage, I'll be able to show the art-work off to my long-suffering coworkers, and I'll have to revert back to the quickness of the Keurig coffee-maker in the morning instead of my comforting, but time-consuming, French press.

But I'll always remember the view.

Why I Wrote This

Good question! My wife is the one who is more in-clined to the written arts, while I once asked a college professor if I could turn in an essay in bullet format. However, I've been enjoying her ability to articulate the ideas she has in her head for many years now. In fact, she's the one who introduced me to Sundial and has even had her own writings on it before.

Despite my avowed engineer nature, I do enjoy doodling and sketching, and she encouraged me to take an online art class during the pandemic. One of the things the class taught me is that anything can be a scene, no matter how common or mundane. I began to look around my house, imagining how things would be drawn. Eventually I looked out my window and saw that a tree formed a "Y" and that it nicely complemented my neighbor's rectangular house.

My train of thought continued and I had this nice mental image of the tree through the seasons when I realized I didn't have that image out of any other win-dows. I wrote down my thoughts and promptly forgot about it for a few months. When I found it again I thought, "Hey, this is perfect for Sundial!" And here I am!

July 19:
Rose Battle

I was born into a very large family. My father had nine siblings and my mother had seven. They married. We had an army of support growing up in the

home our father built for us in the woods on "Battle Hill" near Birmingham.

Our Battle family's life was centered on sports and politics. Our home life included our parents and the four of us children: Rose, Joe, Bill and Ginnie Battle, and our horse, monkey, dog and rooster.

All my life, I've written poems and stories for myself, and written and illustrated stories for the many

children in our family. I've told stories about "Battle Hill" in the 1940s and 1950s, as well as "Granny Stories" about our mother's mother. I do this to preserve our joys, our Southern ways, and words.

Nine years ago, I began appearing on WEUP Radio on "The 50 Yard Line," a call-in sports show.

Thirteen years ago, I first tried out to be on WLRH Public Radio. I've loved telling my stories on the *Sundial Writers Corner*. It has led me to many opportunities to achieve my goal of sharing the great parts of growing up Southern.

My father would reply to any idea I had by saying, "Throw it out there, Sister Baby. Let's see if you have any takers."

So I have, and I am.

She Don't Do Nothing

One of the children I tutored was a third grade Spanish girl named Rosie. Rosie's mother, Alma, came from a very well-to-do Spanish family. Her father, Lief, came from a normal financial situation. Alma would ask me to help her with many things. Her intriguing requests for help always sent me right over to Alma's home—pronto!

One fine spring day, Alma called me and said, "Rosita, my feets are up and she don't do nothing." I drove over right away to decode that request.

Alma told me, as she was lying in bed with her legs and feet straight up in the air, that her doctors told her she was pregnant and she had to put her feet up. She couldn't last much longer, she said.

I told her that he meant for her to rest her whole body flat and just prop up her feet on a pillow every few hours for an hour.

She said, "Gracious Dios!" Then she said, "She still don't do nothing."

I said, "Alma, who won't do anything?"

"The roast, she don't do nothing."

I said, "Where is she?"

Alma put her "feets" down on the floor, and said, "She is in the oven, but she don't do nothing. Every time I look, she won't do nothing."

I looked in the oven. It wasn't turned on at all.

I showed her how to turn on the oven, how to set the timer, and how to get the roast out of the oven, and how to turn off the oven, because Alma did not have her house helpers here in the good, old USA.

Alma thanked me and said she had to go put her "feets" up. She said, "If she does something, I will call you, and we will bring you some roast beef."

I never got that call. I guess "She don't do nothing."

July 26:
Pashka Konstantinow

I'm a college student currently living in Huntsville, Alabama with my mom and little sister. We've lived in five different states (including Alaska)! I love traveling

to different parts of the world, being outdoors, and spending time with my friends and family. When I'm not busy working or studying, I love to sit down and write. Although writing is only a hobby of mine, it is one of my favorite things to do, and I love the creative outlet for self-expression that it provides!

My Brief but Spectacular Take On...

Embracing the inevitable. I feel like the things that make people most unhappy in the context of life as a whole, is the fact that so many things are so inevitable. It is impossible to avoid aging, arguing with our loved ones, failing at things we want so badly to succeed at; these are just basic things that happen in life, and there is little we can do to completely prevent them. While I don't believe we should ever give up on the things we care about, I realize that there is a lot of peace to be found in embracing that which we cannot change. Look for the bright side in all circumstances, even the ones that seem most hopeless. We know they are going to happen regardless, so we might as well enjoy the lessons, experiences, and blessings that inevitably accompany these inevitable things.

The Bridge Across the Sea

I love the way the reflection of the sun creates a bridge across the sea. A glimmering stretch of pure light that connects the solid ground to the mystery of the horizon we could never reach. If I could walk across this radiant structure of gleaming water, I would walk forever; for it is impossible to catch the horizon. It is always miles away; an enigma, a destination we cannot reach at the end of a bridge we cannot cross. Gazing longingly out at the vast ocean, I allow my mind to wander. If the horizon never moved, and the reflection of the sun on the water could hold me, I would run away from all that is here. On the glowing expanse my feet would fly as the beach and all that it held vanished behind me. I would become one with the wind and sun and sea: lost in the mystery. There would be no pain, no love, no memory; I would forget and be forgotten. I would cease to exist. The bliss of that experience would be the death of me, but from where I stand alone on the beach I do not care. I am aware only of my gravity. Gravity to the earth, to my life, to my memories, and to my pain. I cannot escape and I never will, because the horizon is eternally unreachable and the reflection of the sun on the water cannot hold me and my overwhelming gravities.

Why I Wrote This

I wrote this piece to illustrate the longing to escape the heaviness of life that so many people experience. I got this idea a few years ago when I was walking past a lake near my house and noticed how the sun reflected perfectly across the water. When I approached the edge, the reflection seemed to disconnect from the shore and drift further away. I imagined what would happen if someone were able to catch it before it drifted away. This concept of running away from reality and the responsibilities of adulthood on a glimmering make-believe bridge inspired me to write this. I like to visualize the narrator as a tired, worn-out person who is burdened by their job, relationships, and past experiences. Even though they know they must carry on, they allow themselves a moment to fantasize a world where none of these things mattered; an eternal child-like state of peace and sunshine.

July 29:
Amelia Rathz

My name is Amelia Rathz. I have a dog, a gerbil, a hermit crab, and four fish. As you can probably guess, I love animals. In addition to taking care of my pets

and writing, some of my favorite hobbies include drawing, crafting, and shopping (if that even counts), and playing my clarinet in the Grissom High School Band. I also love reading manga. A couple of my favorite series include *My Hero Academia* and *Toilet-bound Hanako-Kun*. I'm very interested in Japanese and French cultures and would love to visit both countries someday!

My Brief but Spectacular Take On...

Something small that can completely change how you view yourself. It might be a subtle thing, but it makes a huge difference. It happens when you say, "I can't do that." Many times, my friends have looked at my drawings and then said that they can't draw, or they read some of my stories and then joked that they can't write. This isn't true at all, and I don't think it's ever funny to joke about self-doubt. Anyone can pick up a pencil and draw, even if it doesn't look good at first. It's the same for writing, reading, playing a sport, singing, or anything you want to try. It makes a difference when you switch your mindset to thinking you just haven't tried enough yet, instead of believing you'll never be good at that activity. Even just admitting you're not good at it right now can help you be more honest with yourself than saying you just can't do it. It's not that you can't, but that you haven't tried enough yet. So, don't give up!

Future Nova

Clink! Evony's tools flew through the air as she fin-
ished adjusting her latest invention. It was no longer
a far-off fantasy — she was holding a time machine.
Evony had made it in the portable form of a belt to
satisfy the year of 2322's popular trend of compact
devices, so it was surprisingly heavy for its size. With
a vain smile, Evony flipped her long pink hair out her
face and imagined her friends Arina, Roman, and
Ven's reactions when she showed her device off at
their weekly invention club meeting today. Just last
week Roman had bet Evony she would never be able
to complete it. Of course, he was just joking. Roman
wouldn't hurt a lightfly. But, Evony never backed
down from a challenge, and when she got to the club
meeting today, her friends would be showing off their
silly, useless little contraptions while she showed them
the most incredible thing they would ever see in their
lives.

Not that she'd let them use it. No, Evony intended
to go back in time and fix all her past mistakes with
the time machine belt. She would be a perfect human
being — not that she thought lowly of herself in the
least — but Evony was still thrilled by the idea. She
planned to stop wars and become an honored queen
for millennia to come. Perhaps she could even-- with
an expression similar to that of a wet cat, Evony real-
ized she was late for the invention club meeting. She
grabbed her bag and went to dash out the door when

a strange whirring sound made Evony practically jump out of her skin.

A girl who looked exactly like her was standing in her living room. Evony screamed. "*Who are you? An imposter?*" Evony growled at her double.

"No, you idiot. I'm you," the girl said, "I'm Evony, and I know you're Evony too. I don't have time for this. If you need some explanation...'" She held up a device identical to Evony's time machine belt.

"How did you?" Evony scrounged around inside her bag until she realized what the other Evony had done. "You used *my* device?"

The girl sighed. "As I said: I'm you from the future. You can call me Nova for now since *clearly,* you can't understand that I'm you and you're me and all that. Look, I need to tell you something." Evony closed her eyes and took a deep breath before deciding that this was for the best. She could just bring Nova along to the restaurant for the club meeting, and then she would have perfect proof that the time machine worked. This realization also made Evony remember that the club meeting would have started exactly fifteen minutes ago.

"Fine. Tell me. And be quick about it too." Evony snapped.

Nova blinked, took a breath, and uttered two words: "Roman's dead."

There was silence. Evony didn't know how to react to this news. Her friends were the only people she cared about other than herself. Evony wanted so badly to believe that Nova was lying, but here the facts were, laying themselves down in front of her.

"How?" was all Evony could manage, her arrogant smile gone.

"I don't know. I left the restaurant to go get my bag and the time travel machine from the vehicle, and when I came back... he was gone. I didn't know what to do, so I used the belt." Nova was ghostly white recalling the nightmare of an experience.

"Wait." Evony gasped. "You said the restaurant. As in tonight's club meet? We can still save him from whoever killed him. It had to be someone at the restaurant, right? If we can keep an eye on Roman the whole time we can stop the murder before it happens."

Nova nodded. "If we can save him in the past, he'll return to my future, but there's a catch: If I don't return to the future before the time here ends up at the time that I left at, I'll disappear. There can't be two of the same person when the times converge. We have to stop the murder before eleven thirty-two."

"Great. As if we needed any more pressure." Evony rolled her eyes, and the two ran out the door.

Evony and Nova arrived at the Eternity Diner five minutes later and slipped in through the revolving door. Inside, a group of three teenagers was loudly chattering at a high-top table. The hanging decorations in the Eternity Diner shone with sparkly light, and the tabletops glowed like the moon. Arina, the girl with the long purple hair and the orange dress turned around and spotted them. Evony ducked behind a chair, realizing she needed to figure out how she would explain the copy of herself to everyone in the restaurant. They had left so fast that she and Nova hadn't even thought of putting a disguise on one of them. Confusion wasn't something else they needed right then. Arina waved over Nova who reluctantly went over to their table with a glance back in the present Evony's direction.

Nova sat down across from Ven, the awkward, quiet kid who was fiddling with a little button he must have invented. Nova stared at him suspiciously, before turning her eyes to . . . Then, Nova saw him. Roman was sitting there next to Ven and was talking to Arina about the small bracelet teleportation device she had made. His bright blue hair was hard to miss as it clashed with his yellow eyes and his blue washed-out tee. Nova's eyes filled with tears at the sight of her friend.

Don't cry. Don't cry. Don't cry. Evony prayed from the next booth over where she was silently watching her friends like a hawk. But, the worst part was that Evony knew herself too well. She couldn't even imagine how awful it would be to see a friend who had died just a few hours ago come back in someone else's world. Although normally she would never cry in front of others to spare her ego, Evony had a hard time holding in her feelings when something bad happened.

Nova stood up, lying that she had to go to the restroom, and slid into the booth with Evony. Wiping her eyes, Nova looked away from her past self in embarrassment. Evony pushed down the feeling of shame at her future self nearly bawling her eyes out and ruining everything.

"We only have about ten more minutes, and I haven't seen any weird behavior so far," Nova whispered to Evony, nervousness now adding to the grief written all over her face. Evony agreed, looking equally panicked. Nothing out of the ordinary had happened. And they were cutting it really close at this point. As if on cue, a horrible sound like a siren mixing with a scream from Arina filled the room.

Nova and Evony both jumped up, but Nova, remembering that one of them had to stay hidden, quickly dove back down and peeked around the side. The teleportation bracelet device was glowing with a bright light and seemed to be emitting the noise. Arina covered her ears and backed up from it.

"What's happening to it?" Evony shouted over the noise, though it seemed to be getting a bit quieter. Roman and Ven looked terrified, and they too had to raise their voices to be heard.

"It was just lying here and then…" Ven started, but he trailed off not knowing what happened, and looked at Arina confused.

"I must have wired it wrong. Or when Roman and I were playing with it, a wire must have snapped. If it's making this noise that must mean it is going into manual mode. Th-that basically means that if someone doesn't put it on, we'll all get teleported into nothingness by the time the sound disappears. Basically, we all die." Arina frantically explained.

"And if someone puts it on... what then?" Evony asked, dreading the answer.

"If someone puts on the bracelet, then they will disappear." Arina's voice wavered. Roman hung his head ashamed. He was visibly shaking from head to toe.

"I should put it on. It was me who broke it. I snapped the side wire when I was looking at it the first time." As a pale-faced Roman went to put on the bracelet, to disappear from reality forever, Evony suddenly realized what had happened to him in Nova's timeline. He hadn't been inside because he'd been teleported into nothing. It wasn't murder. Roman had sacrificed himself to save his friends.

"*NO!*" shouted a voice. Everyone turned to look over at Nova, who had appeared from her hiding place. Roman froze.

"Wait, why are there two Evonys?" he asked, confused. The noise was steadily getting quieter. It was now about the sound of a whistle.

"There's no time to explain," Nova said. "Evony, I have to do this. My time is only one minute away. If I try to go now, I know I'll regret it." Evony stared back at her in astonishment, all dislike of the other girl vanished.

Suddenly, without waiting for a response, Nova snatched up the bracelet from the table, which was now barely audible, and slid it around her wrist.

"Nova, why?" Evony screamed, her eyes filling with tears, as a light as bright as the moonlit sky surrounded her future self.

Nova gave a small, sad smile and said, "Because, Evony, I live on as long as you do. We are the same person."

Then, Nova was gone.

Why I Wrote This

Originally I had intended for my short story "Future Nova" to be a full-length novel with a more complex plot and even more characters, but I have always had a hard time getting all of my story ideas into the written text, so I put the idea on hold for a while. In the original story line, my protagonist Nova was going to be accused of killing her friend Roman, and somehow it was also supposed to be a rom-com. Later that month, I had to write a short story for my English Honors class, and my idea for the sci-fi time travel drama came back to me. I ended up rewriting "Future Nova" as a short story, and I was surprised by how it all came together in the shortened version. When the Huntsville Literary Association's 2021 Young Writers Contest started accepting entries, my GHS English teacher recommended that we submit our stories. I revised my story a lot before submitting it to the contest, and I'm happy with how it turned out.

© 2021 Amelia Rathz

August 2:
Melissa Ford Thornton

Born in Redondo Beach, California, Melissa Ford Thornton earned her M.A. at the University of Alabama in Huntsville. She is Communications Director  for the historic Princess Theatre Center for the Performing Arts in Decatur, AL, as well as a professional storyteller, podcaster, mental health advocate, poet and music lyricist.

Melissa has shared true tales on big stages, bringing a gentle mix of quirky humor and poignant imagery to live audiences at *The Moth*, *Arc Stories*, *Tenx9 Storytelling*, *Stories Under the Stars* and *Tin Can Stories*. Her work has been published by *Silver Birch Press*, in *Good Grit magazine* and frequently airs on WLRH public radio. In 2019, Melissa published a collection of poetry and prose: *An Elegant Dispute of the Accidental*.

My Brief but Spectacular Take On...

On my eleventh birthday, I was gifted a journal. The cover - soft vinyl and heart-shaped - was clasped with a tiny lock and key. The pages within were unlined. I dutifully began filling blank white space with my crooked and cramped handwriting snaking across the page as if I were riding a roller coaster while capturing thoughts. Then and there, I recognized I vehemently dislike unruled paper.

Thus began my life-long love affair with the ruled page. I adore the faint blue lines carefully marking off in even increments where writing *should* be placed. I enjoy the red vertical margins demarking the boundaries meant to contain every word. And nothing gives me more pleasure than setting pen to paper defying every rule. In messy fashion, my still-cramped all but illegible writing wanders across the page jumping past margins, squeezing words below, above and between blue hashmarks. Free form and disorderly, this is how hopes and thoughts move from my imagination to become tangible. This is why my heart-shaped, soul thoughts will always be recorded on ruled paper.

Never Feed a Bear

I was seven the day my brothers and I learned life as we knew it was no more. Poof! Gone.

Dad's firm transferred him to the New Mexico mountains. *From Los Angeles.*

Living within watermelon seed-spitting distance of LA's beaches, we were born with sand between our toes and city lights in our eyes.

Cloudcroft, New Mexico was 9,500 feet above sea level, home to *almost* 500 souls (during peak ski season). The library was a dented camper that arrived from Albuquerque every other week causing quite the stir.

If you're wondering what we were doing there – so were we. Dad's new assignment involved tracking satellites with a powerful telescope in an Observatory. The entire point was to be as far from city lights as possible for clear images of space.

The Lincoln National Forest rose all around us. This is where Smoky the Bear became poster mammal for the "Only YOU Can Prevent forest fires" campaign. Smoky was cute. But the black bears roaming the edges of Cloudcroft? Not so much. Posters in the Post Office and General Store warned: "DON'T FEED THE BEARS!" Dire tales circulated of chickens eaten alive – screen doors clawed.

I know, this sounds exciting.

But we didn't know how to ski. There was no movie theater within 100 miles. For "entertainment,"

Dad bundled us into Mom's Station Wagon and drove to the Dump. Yes – where trash rots.

There's no darkness like a moonless mountain-night dark. The car's high beams focused on the trash pit. Fascinated, we watched a massive mama bear and cubs materialize. They foraged through potato peelings, soup cans and steak bones – their musky, primal odor seeped through the heater vents and we shivered. Fingers crossed, hoping our scent: human fear – thinly disguised as awe and wonder – carried upwind.

That night I dreamed a bear ate my stuffed animals.

But bears hibernate. Spring arrived. Mom taught school. My brothers joined the track team. Our whole family learned to square dance. (I'm not proud of that).

Mornings, mom scrambled to get four kids out the door earlier than necessary for students but essential for teachers. Our weekday routine involved burnt toast and mom's hollers: "If you're not ready in 2 minutes, I'm leaving!"

Until the morning I woke to a house gone silent. My parent's room was empty. My brothers' rooms – empty. The driveway – EMPTY! The Station Wagon was GONE!

I threw my parka on over pjs - flew out the door and down the rutted road toward town. It was eerie. No human activity the entire 3-mile trek. But tractor trailers lined the highway leading out of town.

My mind, trying to make sense of things, landed on: Bears had invaded town! We were evacuating! (I *was* only seven).

Panicked. I hopped on the running board of the first truck stopped at the red light. Through snot and tears I informed the driver – Bears are coming! I know . . . you just concluded I was kidnapped. But *I'm* telling this story – let's not get ahead of ourselves.

The truck driver, named Hal (I know you were wondering) – drove to Cloudcroft's lone diner. The owners knew him. They knew everyone.

It wasn't yet 5 a.m. when the waitress phoned, jarring Mom from her first sip of coffee. "You missing a little girl?" Mom laughed – no. Then, horrified, she noticed my parka missing.

We sat in the diner, mom's hair askew, while I sipped cocoa and folks gathered to hear about the girl who "saved" their town.

A morning that began with terror ended in relief and laughter. Seems while I was running through a not-yet-awakened town, Mom was driving my brothers to a track meet. That day our family discovered small towns have big hearts. Hearts that want to ensure their neighbor's kids arrive home safely.

By summer, we moved to another small town in Alabama. It wasn't the beach, but we now understood in a place where everyone knows your name -folks stick together – come high water . . .or bear invasions.

Why I Wrote This

As short as our time was in New Mexico, it looms large in my memory and holds a special nostalgia for me. Family plays a central role in much of my writing. And this was the last place my entire family of origin lived under the same roof. My oldest brother left for college just prior to our move away from Cloudcroft.

The town itself was a study in contrasts for us. A small town with a tiny population versus Southern California sprawl; snowy mountains rather than sandy beaches and endless summer. Cloudcroft's slow pace and lack of obvious entertainment bored my brothers and me at the time. Yet our dad's work in an observatory tracking satellites and gazing into the galaxy fascinated us. This is where I first learned, the most exciting things are often spun from ordinary thread turned silken by the imagination. The imagination of a 7-year-old can run rampant when faced with a dark forest, fear of being left behind and dangerous wildlife. Though not everyone has run in fear from a bear invasion, I knew that this was the stuff of story — the inspiration behind my Sundial piece: "Never Feed a Bear."

August 9:
Aparna Bhooshanan

I was born in Huntsville, Alabama in 2004. I grew up in the tranquil city of Madison playing abundantly in its parks and fields. I am a senior at Bob Jones stand-ing at the thresh-old of college. My innate love of languages took me to X'ian, China on an immersive study abroad scholarship pro-gram, sponsored by the US De-partment of State. Later, I parlayed that experience into volunteering as a teacher in an English as a Second Language (ESL) program at a local church serving a broad swath of the local community. I plan to study computer science in college. My pastimes include reading, writing, learning languages, and playing with my very stinky bichon.

My Brief but Spectacular Take On...

Being vulnerable. It's so easy to call ourselves mature for closing off and refusing to share our troubles with our friends or family, but sometimes all you need to feel better about something is to share it with someone close to you. If I hadn't shared my identity struggle that I wrote about in this piece with my family, I would probably still be wrestling with it today.

I Matter Because...I too, Am American

Last year, I won a study abroad scholarship funded by the State Department to study Mandarin Chinese. The program was executed by a non-profit called National Security Language Initiative for Youth (NSLI-Y). Since I could remember, I had always been enraptured by this ancient language of mellifluous tones and natural lilts. As a non-Chinese speaker, I found its cadence puzzling, yet admirable. I had opted for that choice in my application. For the first time in my life, I traveled out of the country without my parents along with a group of about twenty other high school students from across the U.S. I was incredibly fortunate to stay with a host family in one of the oldest cities of mainland China called Xi'an in the Shaanxi province. The six-week immersion program for American high school students enabled us to develop a working knowledge of Mandarin.

It was there in that summer of 2019 in Xi'an, at the age of fifteen, that I had to confront the question of my intersectional identity and why it mattered. The most trying challenge I was forced to digest was the perception many natives had of me. As I passed people on the streets, I often heard conspicuous chatter about my skin tone and speculations about my nationality. No matter what language they first heard me speak, natives' default label for me was "Indian."

It was not necessarily a jarring experience; I had traveled frequently abroad before, and in every country, I have visited, people have mistaken me for having been a native-born Indian. In China, as I was alongside people of many races, the difference in treatment was blatant. Chinese American students were spoken to in rapid-fire Chinese, and they were often given disappointed or confused looks when their conversational Mandarin was stretched too thin with a native speaker. African American students were subjected to the prodding of passersby who, on some occasions, touched their hair as they simply walked down the streets. Brown students were admired for their large eyes but pitied for their darker skin. And white students were hailed as beautiful, light-skinned Americans, as it was of them whom the natives first pictured when they heard "美国人." (American). Comparing my experience to that of white students', I came to the realization that no matter where I went in the world, people first saw me as an Indian. It was there, in China, that I first grappled with this question: Where on Earth am I truly American?

I remember an evening dinner at a grand restaurant with my host family and their relatives. One gentleman in the group kept on repeating annoyingly that I was not American-- not knowing that I had picked up sufficient Chinese to understand what he was saying. I kept looking in his direction until it clicked that I had followed his conversation. The feeling was deeply gratifying to me that I could understand a native speaker, but understanding the content was also one that filled me with unease and disquiet.

For a time, I was uncertain how to approach this subject. Calling the standard of one's own nationality is, after all, an unusual situation. I felt a dissatisfying urge to crowd any semblance of Indian culture into the deepest recesses of me and, instead, allowed my more concentrated American side to percolate about my mind in some sort of spiteful cultural ablution. I wished to purge myself of any traces of the country which had endowed me with my skin, and the country that I felt had imbued the doubts and speculations that presently haunted my shadow. This enterprise did not end well, or even make it to completion; Indian culture is dear to me, however fractionally present it may be in me. Attempting to tamp it into a corner only made it come more alive, amplifying the facets of it that I missed sincerely. I continued to wrestle with the question by assessing it from the perspectives of others: I concerned myself with how people's perception of me shifted, or didn't, the farther I traveled, and I wondered how I could wrench this perception from their eyes.

One day, while out with my friends at the legendary Huimin Jie market, something happened when I had just finished bartering for a necklace, I had bought for my host sister. I was hoisting my backpack onto my shoulder when an elderly couple approached the stall.

"How much?" they asked the vendor, pointing to the necklaces. They spoke with an accent I placed as some sort of Mediterranean lilt.

"你想要哪个?" the vendor asked. *Which do you want?*

"What?" they asked. The wife was irritated. "Speak English, please."

"She is asking which one you want," I offered a translation, smiling. I had pushed down my nerves to assist them. They returned my smile, and the wife held up a necklace.

"This one," the wife said. I turned to the vendor.

"他们要这个," I told her, gesturing to the necklace they had chosen. *They want this one.*

"好，三十块," she responded. *Thirty yuan.* I turned to the couple and relayed the information.

"But I can try and make it go lower than that," I grinned. "How much would you like it for?"

"Ten yuan, please," they said, and I turned back to the vendor, beginning to barter. I got the price down to fifteen yuan, but after that, the vendor did not budge.

"Thank you so much," the couple told me after they paid the money and took the necklace. I hastily told them it was my pleasure before seeking out my American friends who had begun moving away from the vicinity.

After I found them, I felt a hand on my shoulder. I whipped around, ready to guard my backpack, but when I turned, I was met by the elderly couple I had left not a minute before. I smiled in relief.

"Hello!" I beamed.

"Hello," the wife said, touching my hand. "We did not get to thank you well enough earlier."

"Are you from India?" asked the husband.

"No," I said, "I am from America." I was not offended; it was a common mistake, and I had become desensitized to it by now in China, even if it still hurt to think that some did not hear my accent and instantly know that I was American.

The husband leaned back on his heels and grinned at me, laughing. "No, you are from Greece, now!"

"I am honored," I told him, my heart swelling. "Thank you so much."

Soon, I was swept away by my friends who insisted on going to one of the stores deep within the bowels of Huimin Jie. I followed them, waving goodbye to the couple before turning away. But I would think about the Greek couple for the rest of the day and marvel at that chance meeting.

That delightful encounter made me realize that I had been observing the problem of my own worth as an American incorrectly the whole time. I had to tackle the problem from my own perspective. The charming Greek grandfather was ready to welcome me into his fold. I realized soon after that my American identity, with its intersectionality, does not limit me in any way. Conversely, it makes me malleable to greater diversity.

The answer to my question "Where am I American" then, is this: everywhere. My Americanness does not wax or wane with the ability of foreigners or, even natives, to recognize it. One's nationality is impossible to expel, even if one wishes to cast it away. It is like the creases upon a human palm, which are notched into the hand during gestation, while the skin is like soft nougat. The baby's clenched hand abrades deeper and deeper the canyons of the palm, which are then stamped doggedly into permanence. After birth, the narrow trenches we carve into our palms are visible, and try as one might, we cannot remove them, or sculpt new ones, for our skin is no longer soft or suggestible. Similarly, one's nationality is impressed ineffaceably into one's demeanor, one's speech, and one's philosophies, all while the mind is still soft and impressionable. After maturation, like the marks upon one's palms, it becomes difficult to wash one's hands of it. With this revelation, the solution aligned into my focus. As the French writer, Proust said, "The real voyage of discovery consists not in seeking new landscapes, but in having new eyes."

Why does my identity matter to me? Because by virtue of my birth and upbringing, I matter as American first, and while my intersectional cultural identity may not make this obvious to the world, I know that I am firmly entrenched as American. The sole recognition of this truth has convinced me that despite everything, *I matter*. I will always be a native perennial in this lovely Alabama landscape.

Why I Wrote This

During my sojourn in China in the summer of 2019, my American identity was questioned over and over. While this unsettled me, I reflected on it, and wrote this piece.

.

August 16:
Allen Berry

I moved to Huntsville in 1993, fresh out of college. One night, I stood atop Monte Sano Mountain looking down at the city and said to myself, "This is *my*

town." I worked various TV jobs, before eventually returning to graduate school in 2006. Three years later, I left town for good, or so I thought. I pursued a Ph.D. at USM's Center for Writers but once I got my sheepskin and funny hat, I came back. Huntsville's gravitational pull was just *too* strong. Since then, I've published four books and I'm happy to say, "Huntsville is *STILL* my town."

My Brief but Spectacular Take On...

Teaching creative writing. There is a great line from the old Michael Douglas film *Wonder Boys*, where Douglas tells a young, budding author: "You can't teach a writer to write. You can teach him what you know and let him find his own way." And that, my friends, is the entirety of what you need to know about learning to write. There is simply no one sure way in. Like a Zen monk would tell you, we must all find our own path. The best I can give a student—the best ANY writing teacher can give a student—is habits of mind, practices, and a few strategies for wooing the Muse so that she lends you her favors. My best advice: read a lot and broadly, take risks, live life boldly, and then—and *only* then— once you've done all that, sit down to write. Anything else is defrauding your readers.

Poems About Love and Loss

Disappearing Acts

It was a Wednesday
so the historians
tell us, when a
Canadian Brigantine
found the good ship
Mary Celeste
empty and adrift
but seaworthy.

And it was likely
a Monday in Virginia
when "croatoan"
was found carved
on the trunk
of a tree.
The Anasazi left
no forwarding
address, no note,
not so much as
a Dear John
when they went.

So I guess
it only makes
sense that
one Saturday
you vanished

completely
from my life.
After all,
you were
always
a stickler
for tradition

Tuesday, Defunct

The Commodore 64 sleeps
in the back of my childhood
closet, on a shelf next to
my Nokia flip phone,
your number still
on speed dial, or
your number from 2005

Some nights, when
I'm feeling nostalgic,
I take out my Nintendo,
blow on the cartridge,
play Mario Kart, while
listening to the hits
of 2008 on my Zune.

Entropy catches up
with everything, but
planned obsolescence
can't lay a glove on
my nostalgia,
so it is…

years and miles away,
on a quiet Tuesday night
I realize I long ago served my purpose
but there are times,
I still miss your touch.

Why I Wrote This

A colleague of mine recently commented, "Nobody writes when they're feeling happy!" In my case, it is an unfortunate truth: life starts going well, and the work suffers; sadness and suffering lead to creativity and fresh work. In fact, a few years ago I taught a workshop at a writer's conference called "Making Pearls: Turning Pain into Poetry" in which I advised poets to take the thing that hurt them, and write about it, then put it away, then visit it later with fresh eyes.

Unfortunately (or fortunately depending on how you look at it), my poetry is often pain plus time. That is not to say that my poetry is purely therapy, but it does help. Nothing gets wasted, nothing gets discarded. These two particular poems are a response to that little voice at the end of every bad break up that asks "Why?" and "What about all the experiences we didn't get to have together?" Mostly, these poems get to say what the poet didn't... for the poet and for any reader who had unused love festering in the aftermath.

© 2021 Allen Berry

August 23:
Joyce Billingsley

I had the good fortune to grow up in Yorkshire, England, in a very stable family. Marrying an American soldier created a complete turn in the road and a mul-

titude of blessings. For the next twelve years we traveled around the globe and had two daughters among war and separations. Every experience made me resilient and mostly optimistic. I like to say that it was never boring and even on my own now I especially appreciate family. I realized along the way that life stories mustn't be lost so I started to write down those I've gathered. Everyone has stories and if reading or hearing any of mine make people remember and value their own then I've succeeded.

My Brief but Spectacular Take On...

Covid has hijacked our world. For those who are lucky enough to survive, I'm thinking it's creating a permanent seismic shift. It's like a world war because of the catastrophic and irreplaceable loss of lives leaving so many families grief-stricken and permanently maimed. Masks are now a part of our wardrobe as were gas masks in Great Britain during World War II. Group activities ceased and people stayed home behind blackout curtains. We're all experiencing empty shelves, shortages, and, at times, rationing.

I know that wars also create discoveries and advances such as new ways to treat the sick. And don't forget society changed forever when women went to work while their men were at war. There was no putting that genie back in its bottle. If Covid had come in the 20th century, I fear it would have created a worldwide traumatic decline in our civilization. The biggest blessing is that technology is advanced enough so that many people can work from home and kids can access schools remotely. We may be staying home but there's the internet, Zoom calls, Facetime, emails and texting. These are new ways to communicate, some that didn't exist until recently. Equally important, we've been offered hope when scientists rapidly developed vaccines and the medical profession has palliative care.

While I accept that at my age staying home and slowing down are a natural process I do wonder what this new world order will bring about for all the younger generations. It's bound to create some very profound changes. Some we can already see but so many we have yet to learn. My hope is that everyone will use this time to realize the importance of being connected to family and friends. It's crucial that we retain our very best human traits of kindness and compassion. If families can learn to get along together, appreciating one another's differences instead of squabbling over them. We all need each other more than ever before.

Heat Spots

School summer holidays in my childhood included staying a week with my aunt. My mother was from a farming family and had brothers who were farmers and butchers. Most lived around the town of Skipton in Yorkshire. It's known as the gateway to the dales which is so picturesque that it's a designated National Park. Mum's only sister ran a boarding house there. I grew up visiting all the Skipton family so I knew my way around. I had aunts, uncles, and cousins galore within walking distance of Auntie Eva's boarding house where I stayed. So I became a regular visitor in the summers from around 8 years of age until my early teens. Back in that era, kids were free to roam alone so I visited the family and ran errands for my aunt.

At the top of the high street was a medieval castle and church and pathways leading into the woods where I loved to walk. Or I'd take Black Walk snicket, a fenced path, that ran alongside the train tracks and came out at the station, a shortcut to Auntie Rose's. To get to my grandmother's house, a lodge at the entrance of a park, I'd go along a scenic canal path and cross over a swing bridge. In the high street I'd wander around shops and market stalls lined up both sides on the cobblestones.

Sometimes I'd get to ride with Auntie Margaret when she delivered meat to customers' homes and other times I'd go into Uncle Joe's or Uncle Eric's butchers shops and watch them make sausages and pork pies. All this meant that Auntie Eva didn't have to worry about keeping me entertained. I had lots of things to do and people to see. She always made me welcome but she was too busy to look after me so sanctioned my gallivanting.

I especially loved sleeping up in her attic. It had a comfy bed and all kinds of interesting odds and ends of furniture, suitcases, dusty Christmas decorations, and bric-a-brac stored around the room. Daylight came in from a couple of small windows in the roof. I would close the door at the bottom of the stairs and be entirely, comfortably alone. It was a cozy, quiet refuge cut off from the rest of the big house. Lying in bed at night, the distant clatter of clogs from the millworkers walking home would ring up from the street, through the open windows, lulling me to sleep.

But in the mornings, I'd sometimes wake up hot and sore from big lumps all over my body. It seemed like every summer I was stricken and when I was hot they itched like crazy. I couldn't say for sure that they began when I was at my aunt's but I associated them with those visits. Over time, my mother and aunt assessed the situation, calling them "heat spots." Likely we'd be "having a heat wave." Or maybe there was "something in the Skipton water?" Most likely I'd brought it on myself by running around the churchyard on a hot day, getting "overheated." Whatever caused it, it was pure misery, a raging itch I turned into a burning fire, heating up my entire body by scratching every welt until it bled. I remember one morning being thoroughly shocked by my red spotted sheet. I must've scratched all night but slept through it.

They tried Chamomile lotion until they ran out so they mixed up baking soda with water and dabbed that on. They bandaged the worst sores hoping I wouldn't infect them. Then they tried home remedies of yellow sulphur powder and syrup mixed into a cloying, gooey mass I swallowed by the spoonful, "to cleanse my system."

Back in school, still scratching incessantly, I remember being a cause of consternation for two teachers who took me out of class. They were probably afraid I had something catching that would put the school in quarantine. I suffered the indignity of one of them pulling the top of my shirt out to peer down inside at my chest and back while the other looked on. I should've been grateful they were so concerned because at home no one seemed to think of taking me to a doctor.

This was apparently an annual occurrence for a few years brought on in summer and took several weeks to disappear. It was an unsolved mystery that eventually went away on its own. The grown-ups said I must have "grown out of it."

It remained a mystery until many years later when I was talking to a cousin about our parents' early lives. Claire laughed about her mother, May, staying, as a young woman, with my mother, her sister in-law, in the old farmhouse and sharing a bed. May was always bitten by fleas overnight while my mother seemed immune. It began to make perfect sense that although I never saw any, fleas might have been in the attic at my

aunt's house. She had a cat that roamed freely out-
doors who liked to sneak to the attic for a nap on the
bed. Auntie Eva didn't approve of cats being upstairs
so it was never there when I was.

Was the timing pure coincidence? I only stayed
with my aunt in summer but as I grew I was allowed
to share her bed in her rather splendid bedroom. I
wonder now if she'd guessed the cause. Whatever,
the "heat spots" didn't appear then. For more than
fifty years it was a long-forgotten puzzle, now pre-
sumably solved.

Why I Wrote This

This story surfaced one hot Alabama summer day when I was thinking about summers in England. In reliving an experience, I surround myself with scenes that capture the atmosphere placing me back in time. Remembering the freedom I had is amazing to me now but it was the norm back then. Since I'm here in the States I realize it will be different from most people's experiences and I enjoy offering glimpses into that world. The fact that this enigma was a mystery for many decades amuses me.

© 2021 Joyce Billingsley

.

August 30:
Michael Guillebeau

My family moved to Huntsville in 1956, when I was 5 years old, and Huntsville, like me, was far younger than it is now. I grew up here, brought a beautiful  New York girl back home, and, with her, raised two beautiful children here. I worked for many years as a software engineer for NASA and the DoD (what could be more Huntsville?) In 2013, I retired to write fiction full-time. Since then, I have published seven novels and over forty stories. If you've got something you've always dreamed of doing, I am the poster child of why you should get busy with it now. The grass really is greener in the land of your dreams.

My Brief but Spectacular Take On...

Love as an old man. Like most people, when I was young, I assumed that at the age I'm at now, love would consist of holding hands on a porch swing and grumbling at the old lady. Instead, my wife/soulmate and I are at the most romantic, wild and passionate period of our lives. Who'd a thunk it? Thank you, Pat. And thank you medical science.

Three Stages of Writing

Tea Cup

The barista watched side-eyed
as the old woman touched my shoulder
like a fading butterfly.

"You hold your cup, dear
by the handle,
keeping the tea away
safely distant and cool."

She loosened my shivering fingers from their grasp-
ing
turned my cup around
and wrapped my fingers
around the moon-white porcelain bowl.

"But the tea, and the cup, both need
to give you their warmth."

For that moment
she cradled my fingers
between the fire-born heat within the cup
and the frail human warmth of her hand.

Then she pulled away and pulled up
her ragged collar and

slipped out the door
back into the cold.

I sat where I always sat
turned my hand
back to the cool handle where the world
told me I belonged.

Thought of that cold world
waiting for me outside.

I turned my warm sweet cup around,
and thanked the old woman
and my tea cup.

Made-up Stories From a Bar

We make up stories
for each other, here

Yesterday
I was a mourner, too sad
to speak past my coming tears.
A foot away
you spoke of dandelion fluff
your lightness tickling
until I smiled.

Today
I was a hunter with no bullets
and you a wild hare
fur standing on end, trembling
from memories of old hunts but
determined not to listen
to your fears until
your softness brushed my hand
for only a moment
gentle as a child's blown kiss
before bounding away.

A hundred nights,
a thousand stories,
a million marks on the unmarked pages of our hearts
made and gladly accepted
until we were
as scarred as the old table

between us.

Tomorrow and tomorrow and tomorrow
I will live to tell
my stories
when you are here
when you are gone.

Offering Books

I set my little books out
in ragged boxes
for you.
If you don't take them,
I add chalk.
Maybe you'll make your own art:
Sidewalk verses, puppy dogs, monsters, bees.
Anything.

I add snacks, parties.
Anything
to reach you.
I set my little books out.

Why I Wrote This

I've been a full-time writer for a dozen years and two million words now, and it's still a mystery how this stuff works. The first poem here is about where writing comes from. I was working in a coffee house when a girl came in and ordered tea. When the barista presented the cup handle-first like any normal person, she turned the cup around and cradled the warm cup in her hand. Why?

The second poem is about writing with a partner. Writers quickly learn that writing is intensely solitary. Just as quickly, they learn that it's impossible to write without a reader in mind. So all writing is done with a reader/partner — whether that partner is across the table from you, or just in your imagination.

The third poem? Anyone who's ever sold books or run a bookstore or a library knows the feeling of begging people to read. As Henny Youngman never said, "Take my book, please."

© 2021 Michael Guillebeau

September 6:
Beth Thames

I started writing stories almost as soon as I learned to read, but I never thought of myself as a writer until I took creative writing classes at the University of Ala-

bama. One of my professors told me I just might have some skill, but I needed to work on my craft. Fifty years later, I'm still doing that.

I've been lucky. I married the right person—my high school and college sweetheart—and we've been lucky to have two children and now two grandchildren. Our house is full of books and papers. (Note to reader: If you love to read and write, marry an English major.)

I've been lucky in my career, too. Working first as a clinical social worker and then as a college English Instructor, I began writing commentaries and essays for NPR's *All Things Considered*. This led to publication in *The New York Times*, *Atlanta Magazine*, *Southern*

Living, Working Mother, and other publications. Eventually, my hometown paper, *The Huntsville Times*, hired me to write a weekly column and WLRH aired my pieces. Thanks to Judy Watters who "discovered me" and taped my stories for *All Things Considered*.

One of the highlights of my writing career was when a D.C. cabdriver and NPR fan recognized my voice from a story I'd done about owning pets. He called me "the Alabama Cat Lady" and reduced my fare.

My Brief but Spectacular Take On...

Music. There was always music in my house when I was growing up, though nobody played an instrument. I was a piano lessons dropout when my teacher, a Greek woman in our Baltimore neighborhood who prided herself on producing excellent students, knew I was not going to make the cut. "You are wasting my time and your money," she told my mother, and the piano sat dusty and unused for a few years. Still, there was music.

My parents had a blond mahogany music cabinet with a turntable. The records went from 78s to 33s to 45s. They played the Big Band songs of the forties—Benny Goodman was their favorite—and sometimes danced in the living room to their special songs: "Stardust" and "Deep Purple." They were graceful dancers. Wherever we moved to follow my father's jobs, there was music. Doo-Wop tunes of the fifties poured out of my sister's red transistor radio. We danced to that beat and played the songs for my parents who sometimes clapped along.

By the time I was in high school, rock and roll and rhythm and blues tunes were always on the Birmingham airwaves. We listened to a blues station out of Chicago, too, and if we tuned our radio just right we could hear the deep, sultry voices of Muddy Waters and John Lee Hooker.

When I left home, I took my record albums with me. They were the soundtrack for moving into adult life with marriage, careers, and children. My parents took one cruise before my father died, and they danced all across the ocean. When I wrote my Sundial piece about The Beatles, I remembered how they liked that boy band, too. I never saw them dance to that music, but maybe they did. Or maybe they are now. I'm grateful for the music and for the parents who kept it turned on.

Sir Paul

Sir Paul is coming to Nashville in November. Thanks to a birthday gift, I'll be there.

The last conversation I had with Paul was brief. I yelled, "Paul!"

He turned his head, nodded, and made a sound like, "Lo," which I thought meant "hello" in a Liverpudlian sort of way.

I was twenty and crossing a busy street in Chicago when I had a vision. Surely that parade of long-haired guys rushing into a luxury hotel couldn't be The Beatles!

Surely those bodyguards, burly types who blocked the way for any curious onlookers wouldn't stop me from getting a bit closer.

But they did. The parade moved on, leaving me and the other starstruck fans on the sidewalk. Had we just seen the most popular band on the planet, or was it an illusion? Someone said maybe they were the decoy band while the real Beatles were in a Yellow Submarine in Lake Michigan, waiting to appear when the crowd was gone.

We dismissed this idea. And we went home and told our parents that we'd seen the Beatles and we grew up and told our children that we'd seen them, too. Now I can tell my grandchildren that I saw the Beatles and my guess is they'll smile politely and ask, "Who?"

And that's a good question. They were a boy band. They were genius lyricists and musicians. They were so daring. Their hair reached their collars at a time when crew cuts were the rule. They were smart-mouthed and glib-tongued. But they could charm listeners of all ages, even our parents.

My father, sometimes shocked at the raunchy R&B lyrics he heard on the Birmingham radio stations, loved the Fab Four and hummed "Fool on the Hill" or "Strawberry Fields." He even gave me money for the newest album, "Rubber Soul."

Everybody has Beatle memories. It seems like Yesterday when I heard that iconic song, but it was long ago in Nashville, when Vanderbilt played Alabama and my friends and I drove home, those sweet notes floating out of the car radio. We didn't have much in the way of troubles yet, but we understood that one day we would, and we'd long for yesterday, just like Paul said.

My daughter's first movie was *Yellow Submarine,* and she was afraid of the Blue Meanies for about five minutes until the movie's happy ending, when we all left the theatre singing "All Together Now." Love, as usual, conquered all.

The Beatles followed my generation through college and into adult life, and now, though Sir Paul is older than I am, he's still out there, and good for him.

I don't think he'll notice me, but if I catch his eye in the sea of thousands at the concert, I'll wave and say, "Lo!" Maybe he'll remember the day he wowed a young fan from Alabama when he saw her standing there.

Why I Wrote This

When our generous children gave us tickets to a Paul McCartney concert a few years ago, the memories of listening to the Beatles in my youth came rushing back. There was another memory, too. I'd actually seen The Fab Four once, walking single file into their hotel. This is the back story: My boyfriend (now my husband) and I worked at Yellowstone Park one summer with other college students. On the long train ride back to Birmingham, we had a two-hour layover at the Chicago train station. When my boyfriend fell asleep on the bench, I stuck a note in his pocket saying I was going for a walk. I popped into the YWCA for a quick shower in the locker room, renting a clean washcloth and towel and scrubbing the train grime away. When I headed back toward the station, there they were. The Beatles. Everyone on the street corner stopped and stared. This was 1965. They were the most famous people on the planet. As I yelled out to Paul, he looked in my direction and uttered a one syllable greeting: "'Lo.'" I never forgot it.

© 2021 Beth Thames

September 13:
Andrew V. Gonzales

Hello! My name is Andrew V Gonzales and I currently (as of writing this biography) live, work, and

play in Huntsville, AL. I earn a roof over my head as an analyst by day and stave off the specter of middle age by night. Pizza, public radio, and local markets are my love language. Co-existing with our planet is my life and I have weathered grocery totes, boxes of glass bottles, a compost bin, and solar panels to prove it. When I'm not indulging or saving the world, I am documenting my life, writing, or (my newest love) reading.

My Brief but Spectacular Take On...

Autumn. I adore Autumn. It is my favorite season. No other time of year graces me with painted leaves, Canadian Geese, and meteorologists' dreams. When it isn't Autumn, I count the days. When it is, I cherish every single one. Trees shed their Summer coats like rose petal showers in a city of marble during some grand celebration lined with thousands of loyal subjects. They take all of my attention. It is brain floss. It is cinematic. It is too beautiful to be real. Before all are bare, they sing songs of Gulf waves crashing on white beaches with the winds on my walks. They're always longer during the Fall. Crisp airs and chilly winds let me bundle up in clothing with secret agent man pockets. I can sit outside and do absolutely nothing on these days and feel zero guilt. I can eat pumpkin pie with more whipped cream than usual and feel zero sin. I wake up every morning feeling like the end of a trilogy where good succeeds and it only needs to make its way home. Autumn is home to me. I was, after all, born in this season.

Sunday School #82

After months of patience, last week finally afforded me the time to conduct one of the most involved overhauls of my personal memories; the analog overhaul.

This overhaul included nine rolls of super 8mm film, five cassettes of magnetic tape, and forty rolls of 35mm film. All, alongside handwritten journals, have been responsible for documenting my life since early 2019. Prior to, I used their digital equivalent.

Writing is the only exception.

Apart from a small divergence in journal #1 (Reclaim), it has always been analog.

With such a legacy in the digital world (five years' worth), it was easiest to store my analog memories with the same convention. I organized by event. I named with date and time. I never questioned the convention until the labors of scale began to reveal themselves (particularly, with 35mm film). A better solution graced my daydreams until it manifested itself in none other than my handwritten journals.

It was a solution born from circumstance that now dictates how I refer to any of my written works. I, like an artist, stole from another and applied the goods to a practice of my own. It changed everything.

Now, every journal carries a name, every entry carries a number, and every paragraph is a verse.

Standing before this elegance, I turned to every other analog medium in my arsenal.

Are rolls of film not volumes of text? Is a stretch of magnetic tape not one entry in a series? Can a scene in a super 8mm film serve as a verse?

The answer led to an action to overhaul. Upon its discovery, I knew I could not immediately accommodate it. I knew it would take a substantial amount of time. A normal workweek afforded none. I needed a week off.

I needed last week.

Volume contents were scanned and processed. Files were renamed and timestamps reconciled. I breezed through the categories of audio and video with only a mild sense of anxiety. The category of photography introduced an entirely new level of despair because of its sheer volume. Yet, all three categories combined did little to prepare me for the effort required to overhaul the final category; writing.

"It will be so involved because I will have to add my entry and verse marker to every journal that has been scanned in at some point. In time, every journal will carry these markings. For now, however, there is no need. The ones on my computer will take enough time as it is. Last evening, I completed this exercise up to where I've shared in my very first journal. It wasn't too bad. Tedious. I ran into a number of complications associated with idiot journaling practices on my part so long ago. It forced me to taint my elegant naming convention. Hopefully, they go extinct (the exceptions). It was an interesting experience [reclaiming] and adding to such old volumes of text. I felt like an archivist retracing the steps of an old civilization. More so, I felt like I was laying the groundwork and infrastructure for future archivists to navigate with. It was as if I was an ancient alien species leaving towering monoliths behind to be found by future explorers and used and interpreted. It is a special moment that I will continue to experience today. I'm setting a foundation that future visitors to my universe will be able to take advantage of for their own journeys.

Towering monoliths... this is what I am building with every pen stroke, every shutter release, and every magnetizing field I summon throughout my life."

— Broadcast 51:16-17

In total, overhauling the selected journals (eight out of forty-three) took fourteen hours. Add in the other categories and a day will have elapsed. I've never been so mentally exhausted.

At the same time, I've never been so proud. I can't help but be in awe when I look back at what I've built. And I cannot wait to see what I have yet to build.

What are you leaving behind?

Here's to a great user manual.

Why I Wrote This

This essay is the eighty-second instantiation of a writing series I called, "Sunday School". Every Sunday, for two years straight, I would read back at a week's worth of journal entries, find the verse (or verses) that spoke most to me, and write about it (or them) on my blog. Each essay included the inspiring verse(s) such that it read seamlessly. Sunday School #82 was inspired by a massive overhaul of how I organize and store all of my life's records and the monuments I realized I was leaving behind throughout.

September 20:
Rosemary McMahan

I have loved poetry since childhood, going on to earn a BA and MA in English Literature. After teaching English at UAH, I eventually became an ordained

minister in the Presbyterian Church, crafting sermons instead of poetry. When I semi-retired in 2020, I had the space to write poetry again.

My poetry has been published in several journals, and I've been awarded two state Hackney Literary Awards. Yet what I value most about writing are the monthly gatherings with my local poet-sisters.

My husband, Dennis also retired in 2020. Our son and daughter now live too far from home. We are feeling our way through this life transition and re-discovering the simple blessings each new day brings.

My Brief but Spectacular Take On...

Beauty. I doubt anyone would disagree that the last couple of years in the United States have been ugly ones. From politics to pandemic, a harsher, more divisive, side of all of us has been revealed. In the face of so much confusion and upheaval, I have wondered what one action I could take that would make any difference, and I have realized that what matters now, perhaps more than ever, is creating beauty.

Beauty comes in so many forms. It can be found in words, in the poignancy of poetry and prose. It can be found in color when artists are painting and quilters are stitching. Beauty comes from the sculptor's chisel, the musician's instrument, the gardener's green thumb, the photographer's sense of shadows and light. Like the Creator, we are called to create in the midst of this present darkness, our offerings the candles that shine with hope and beauty.

Ritual

Smith Lake, Alabama
April, 2020

Again and again, back and forth,
one after another,
herons skim the lake
from a wooded hillside
to a strip of peninsula
where boughs of pine
bend to their reflection.
Blue-grey wings lift up,
draw down,
again and again,
following a trajectory
of instinct and memory,
back and forth,
against a wind
that stirs the surface of the lake
in eddies, ripples, and shimmers.
The males gather twigs, moss,
reeds, and needles of pine.
Again and again,
the females weave
instinct and memory into nests
within the treetops
above the water
and await the eggs,
pale blue, that carry the hope
of forever.

© Rosemary McMahan

A Lament
Smith Lake, Alabama
January 2021

they stripped the lot where the herons roosted
where the herons roosted is no more
smoke curls from the rubbish pile
on the lot where the herons roosted.

tall pines gave welcome to the herons
where they built nests at the top
but there is no welcome now
it lies smoldering in the rubbish pile.

lies smoldering in red clay razed raw
cratered for the sake of vanity
and prestige which only last as long
as great blue herons do.

the lake that fed the herons along the shore
now slushes against broken bones
of hickory of oak   destroyed
for a better view of where herons once flew
for a better view of where herons once flew.

© Rosemary McMahan

Why I Wrote This

I still remember the winter day we arrived at our lake house, the shock and dismay I experienced when I saw the smoldering lot across from us. Up in the pines on that hilly lot, herons had nested each spring. Now, the pines were gone, all of them. Nothing was left but dirt, nature erased for the sake of a big, new home. In just a few short months, we sold our home there. I couldn't bear to watch other beloved places on Smith Lake give way to bulldozers and backhoes.

My heart aches as we continue to encroach on wildlife and destroy nature. I only hope that we will wake up, that our hearts will turn, and that our grandchildren will be able to enjoy the rich gift of the natural world. These two companion poems are my meager tribute, and heartfelt offering, to the Great Blue Herons.

© 2021 Rosemary McMahan

September 27:
Rebecca Moore

I moved to Huntsville from London in 2009, with my husband and our two daughters. We came to Alabama every spring break; I joked that it was the most exotic

destination we could think of, but really it was just to visit family. I have always loved radio, from Dr. Demento as a child to call in-shows in college and NPR and the BBC, so I was thrilled to be able to join the ranks of the Sundial Writers when I moved to Huntsville.

My Brief but Spectacular Take On...

Hope. My daughter has CHD2 and autism spectrum disorder. Before I knew exactly what her issue was, I had an abiding hope that there was a key to the mystery of who she was and how to reach her. And while there were definitely milestones and improvements, she resolutely stayed her course. As a child with a developmental disorder gets older, the gulf between herself and her neurotypical peers only widens. Over time, I learned to hope differently. Say what you will about Justin Bieber, but the fact that my daughter discovered him independently of me and was caught up briefly in the fandom was to me a hopeful sign that she was connected to the larger world. The name of the perfume, "Someday," speaks to both the false hope of recovery as well as the suggestion that wearing the scent will bring you into a star's orbit. "Someday" is how we all preface our hopes. Hope is cheap, but it is also essential.

Making the Turn

I lost my husband one morning in Costco as we were about to check out. I texted him, then called, then saw him looking for me. We had one of those, "I see you now; you're walking toward me" conversations. I lost him again that evening when he had the stroke. And again, five weeks later, when his organs checked out one by one and he drifted away from us.

He stayed with me in the car for several months. I could feel his shoulder in the empty passenger seat.

It took me almost a year to build Costco back into my routine and when I did, I remembered to go wide on the turn off Memorial Parkway, as Jim had always instructed, hassling me about how I changed lanes too late.

"Will you just let me explain?" Jim said the day of his stroke. And so we sat in the car before going in and I let him break it down. "The only person who could hit you if you go wide early," he said, "is some impatient bastard behind you, like me, who passes you on the right."

He needed to get it out of his system, to leave me with a single paragraph in the unwritten instruction manual for a life without him. That and a bookmarked link for a piece in *The Toast* about how to buy a car without ever having to speak with a human, which I found after I totaled mine at a different intersection the following summer.

Who was I anyway? Had my husband been the interesting, attractive, funny one? Without him, would I still fall asleep listening to podcasts or would I rather routinely stay up until midnight? Would I really be happy eating salad for dinner as he always suspected I would if left to my own devices? "Big salad," he would say, doing jazz hands, imitating how I might try to sell such a meal. "We're just going to have a big salad!"

But after we had eaten the last of the food people brought us and were running out of paper products, there was no avoiding going back. Making the turn was hard. Going wide early as he instructed was the last thing he ever taught me. I've been figuring out the rest as best I can ever since.

Do we really need to keep buying chicken? What will two people do with a bag of avocados? I filled my cart, arms, house with multiples that would exceed my appetite.

In the months that followed his death, Costco's abundance was a reminder of all we were not, did not do, or need. I no longer needed the gigantic box of oats to make the granola he liked, and I stopped buying coffee from the downtown roaster and bought beans in bulk. I cancelled the cable and let them play baseball without us.

We had been a family of four. Soon our younger daughter would leave for college and the older daughter, because of her disability, would be with me forever. She was eager for me to find a replacement husband as soon as possible. "I don't want it to be just the two of us," she said. She offered me up to visitors, cousins who came to the memorial service. "My mom really needs a new husband," she said.

"I don't," I said.

That summer, I met someone. Our daughters had become friends at school and introduced us. We went to Costco together the way a young couple might dog-sit, a trial run for marriage or parenthood. We divvied up the avocados, a two-pack of fancy maple syrup. We cooked more and more meals together. We made plans, big salads. A year later we were married, a family of seven.

At the intersection where you make the wide turn for Costco, there is a Spy Store. Divorce Specialists. Designer concealed carry purses. Bedazzled stun guns. If I had some of their ghost-hunting gear, I could say to him now, You see what I have done? I came back to Costco to resume my life. Do you understand?

Why I Wrote This

I'd like to talk about why I wrote my "Brief but Spectacular Take on Hope." One morning, I was feeling the isolation and dark thoughts of being a special needs parent coupled with the constant attentional demands of parenting. I started writing a private rant, screaming into the void, when our cat jumped into my lap, reeking of Someday, the Justin Bieber perfume. It was one of those comic moments that relieves the ongoing slog of tasks. And then there was a poetic moment in my daughter's special needs yoga class that was the beauty that elevates the experience, that makes you realize there are stars in the darkness. The result was a piece called "Someday," that I read on Sundial in 2015. My favorite moments writing are when the mundane and the mystical bump up against one another to create something extra and unexpected.

October 4:
Cindy Small

Cindy Small, a New Orleans, Louisiana native, suddenly blew into N. Alabama following Katrina. She was born into a Jewish, Viennese family who relocated to The Big Easy from Vienna, Austria. What is so delicious about her Viennese family was that their snobbery and superiority was outmatched only by their neuroses. She had the ability to laugh at the train wreck of her life and arrive all the way to sanity.

Cindy graduated from Tulane University with an undergraduate degree in Journalism and Masters in Historic Preservation Studies.

My Brief but Spectacular Take On...

Always being non-judgmental. While some readers may consider my material outrageous and perhaps over-the-top, my main goal was to open eyes and show that the most unusual childhood can add positive dimensions to one's character.

My stories are unquestionably unique, candid, and totally authentic non-fiction memoirs about my family's relationships between lovers, friends, ex-friends, strangers, and just about anyone their bizarre behavior affected. For me, life with the mafia was all about family and not hardened criminals. I was surrounded by love, laughter, and food and it taught me not to judge people by other pieces of their lives. Embrace the good and absorb all aspects of life with an open heart and kindness. It made me have an incredibly colorful childhood and I am so grateful.

House of Tiki

At six-years old, I loved hanging out with The Dixie Mob. Surrounded by Big Daddies in The Big Easy, my parents and grandparents were regulars at The Candlelight Inn, a crusty old motel located in a vacant parking lot on the outskirts of New Orleans. The exterior of the motel looked like a discount bed-in-a-box with a human-sized flickering, red plastic candle glowing against a dingy neon-yellow sign.

Outside, the air had a mystical smell, sweet olive here, there, and everywhere meshed with the tart-lemony bouquet of magnolias, all New Orleans fragrances. As we entered the motel, I just knew I was inside an ax murderer's house. The thought never occurred to me it was a Big Easy mobster bordello serving scrumptious food.

House of Tiki had spiral stairs in the center of the room. Arriving at the top, you were immediately transported into a party. Decorations were a 50's mix of kitschy Hawaiian Tiki leather furniture and red-velvet, fringed curtains. Men dressed in over-sized suits wearing gold jewelry sat on bar stools.

Long-haired blonde ladies wearing short shorts and sparkly pasties paraded around the floor holding crystal liquor bottles. They poured fine Kentucky Bourbon into the hands of slick pomade-haired men. The men were in deep discussion, smoking thick cigars and grinning through large, yellowed teeth. There was

a stage with thick, floor-to-ceiling steel poles. Shad-
owy female figures gyrated up and down dancing to
'70s disco music.

One of the dancers and also my pal was a hooker
named Psycho-a-Go-Go. Psycho-a-Go-Go was a
beautiful, thin blonde with a Hollywood face and
owned many personalities. Her skin always looked
glittery, and she was the Dixie Mob's favorite. If it
was a good moment, and she had snorted white dusty
powder in the ladies' room, she'd pick me up, and
place me on her shoulders so I could grab the top of
the dancing pole and slide down. Up and down until
I thought a concussion awaited me. She was a female
Atlas.

"Go-Go, please put me down. I is going to throw
up!" I would scream.

"No way, Babydoll. We're gonna do this till the
cows come home and the creek don't rise."

Psycho-A-Go-Go was really nice to me—other
than exposing me to the possibilities of decapitation
but at 6 years old, it wasn't even a thought.

"Come on, Babydoll, faster, faster, faster!!!" Psy-
cho-A-Go-Go would shriek. "I'm just getting' fired
up. Whatza matter wit you, little one? Get this train a
goin'!!!

"Christ, Go-Go, you killin' me!" I'd scream.

But Psycho-A-Go-Go would just yell louder,
"Bounce, Baby, bounce!"

Evening dinners at The Candlelight Inn were about
my family sitting around a large oval table while hand-
some Creole waiters in tuxedos and buxom waitresses

delivered colossal vats of boiling red sauce with meat-balls swimming inside.

I sat on the leopard sofa, drinking fizzing Coke from a frosty Pilsner glass while Big Daddies with huge hands and shiny jewelry dug into their pockets and exchanged rubber-band balls of cash. Deals made in this dim, smoky room along with the aromas of heavy meats and red sauces, kept my family's X-rated lingerie store intact and prospering.

I've come to see that my particular rearing served me much better as a humorous story writer rather than a road map to a normal life. Though my uncon-ventional childhood consisted of playmates like Psy-cho-A-Go-Go rather than a Tiny Tears doll, I man-aged to learn some important lessons and developed my own grit and style. I found commonality with the dancers and waiters and I was one six-year old who could not only disco the night away but shake up a mean Martini. So, in the footnotes of the House of Tiki chapter of my life, I record these lifesaving notes:

- There's always time for lipstick, preferably red.

- Business deals go down better with food, specifically lots of meat sauces and carbs; and

- No matter how shady the setting, there are still good people in the world…but there may be only one and it may be you, so act accordingly and hang on 'til the spinning stops.

Why I Wrote This

Different, unique, and quirky childhoods can produce wonderful experiences even if you do spend time with New Orleans mobsters. I know. That was exactly how I spent my younger years. How much better can it get? The Sicilian food was great, music fabulous, and with strippers teaching me how to disco, I could possibly end up becoming the best dancer in the room. There is literary fodder to be had from friendships with madams, jazz, and mafia dealings.

October 11:
Jackie Williams

At this writing, I am 71 years old and have been married to my amazing husband for 50 years. We have two adult sons. We are both retired from satisfying

careers. Life is good. We make a point of laughing every day.

My Brief but Spectacular Take On...

All families tell stories, whether we call it history, gossip, or an attempt to answer the questions of our children. Our stories distinguish us as individuals but unite us as people. Nothing promotes understanding or restores peace like a good story. Without stories, history would be boring and forgettable; families could have little in common; empathy would suffer; and much of Jesus' best work would be lost.

Going Dial

My hometown had the distinction of being the last area in the state of Alabama to 'go dial.' At that time, there was one phone company. Most families had one phone. Ours was located in the hallway in the center of the house in a niche in the wall made just for that purpose. Prior to 'going dial,' we had a telephone like most in the country, a black boxy phone with the receiver on top. The main difference was that the rotary dial with its white numbers was missing.

When we wanted to place a call, we simply lifted the receiver and placed it to our ear. Almost immediately, a voice said, 'number please.' Sometimes the voice was one of three girls in my class in high school who worked part time as operators. We would say whatever number we wanted followed by please. There were some eccentric callers who might say, 'give me the piggildy wiggildy,' or some other variation, but most calls were by number. My phone number was 1 2 1. I had a friend whose number was 7. When my sister called long distance from California, she often had difficulty making the operator on her end believe that 1 2 1 was the entire phone number.

In addition to placing calls for us, the operators were what we had as 9 1 1 at the time. A customer who yelled 'Fire!' into the phone would get quick results. The same is true for police or Dr. Whoever.

I do not recall ever getting a crank call during that entire decade or so that we had no dial. And I have to think that living with two schoolteachers made as good a target as could be. However, it would have been impossible to be anonymous from the operators.

Having friends as operators had the advantage of requesting a coded ring for certain callers. If, for example, you did not want calls from a certain person, and the ring tone was short, long, short, one could step outside and have one's mother tell that person you were not in without lying. Or so I heard.

When the phone company decided to give dial service to our area, they sent a phone company representative to teach us how to use a dial phone. Most of us had actually made phone calls from other places, so that the new and improved technology was not foreign to us. However, we were given a break from classes to go into the large auditorium, so we were not protesting. This woman, whom I recall as being thin with her hair in a bun and wearing the pencil skirt and jacket identifying her as a woman of business, was placed up on the stage with a table and chair and a phone. I imagine she supplied the phone, as it had a dial. She showed us, as well as she could from that distance, how to dial, and she made the dial tone and busy signal with her voice. Hmmmmm, for dial tone and ah, ah, ah for a busy signal.

I don't actually recall using the dial phone in my home very much, though in a short time, I was away to college where, to my delight, every room had a phone. I do remember meeting two or three people in the following years who worked for the phone company and thus received the phone company newsletter, Upon learning where I grew up, they said, "Oh, the last town to go dial!"

My present phone is smart. It rings a different dial tone for each member of the family; takes and stores pictures; sends and receives emails and texts; gets weather and news; and lets me play games and read books and magazines. And no, I would not trade it for the old black box wired into the wall. But once in a while, when I hear for the sixth time, "Your call is important to us". . . Well, at least I can play solitaire while I wait.

Why I Wrote This

Lily Tomlin made fun of it. Bobby Kennedy broke the monopoly into pieces. But THE PHONE COMPANY was a huge part of life. Phones have not lost their importance. In fact, they are probably more crucial than ever to our young people. But what they have gained in technology, perhaps they have lost in the human touch. My little story about moving into the age of rotary dial is just a speck in the mountain of differences that have happened in my lifetime. I certainly am not a reactionary, but just someone who gives a nod to the past. And I would no more give up my smartphone than I would my microwave!

October 18:
Rhonda Hinkle Broyles

Born in Seattle, WA, in that magical year of 1957 Thunderbirds and rock & roll, I have a yearning for adventure and new vistas. Fortunately, my husband Frank agrees. When I was 5 my family settled in Greeneville, TN. In this small town where guitars and banjos rule, I became a classical bassoonist. I performed for 12 years with the Huntsville Symphony Orchestra, traveled to Gibraltar, canoed the Okefenokee Swamp, hiked to Mount LeConte Lodge (where I thought I might die by the side of the trail), enjoyed three children, many cats and dogs, and many last names. What a trip.

My Brief but Spectacular Take On...

Those who have the ear of the world. If you are fortunate enough to have a platform to make your voice heard to the masses, be you a celebrity, a public servant, or a 15-minutes-of-famer, I beg you, please make your words matter. Make them matter for improving the human condition, or for bringing attention to something we can all join forces in to restore and/or rejoice over, or that we can see as noble, beautiful, and hopeful. I, for one, do not want or need to know the size of your private parts, for example, as I watch political debates where words volley and arch over the needs of the people of the United States of America. I do not want to hear middle school vendettas of who did you wrong and why you're still mad and vengeful.

I am outraged when I see a missed opportunity for someone to speak on behalf of those who struggle beyond measure and beyond our own thinking caps of comfort. I am outraged when I hear mocking of another.

Let's think outside ourselves. To those of you who already do, I thank you. Let's make life better for us all, wherever we are, and for them, wherever they are. Onward!!

Beware Slicky Pajamas

The first I ever heard of the dangers of silky slick (aka slicky) pajamas was when one of my mother's sisters was demonstrating how yet another sister had put on a little silk negligee with plans of a frisky trot across the bedroom to throw herself seductively into the bed with her husband. That was the plan. But once that slicky negligee hit the sheets she had no traction, slid right on past her bewildered husband and off the other side of the bed onto the floor.

That should have been my warning.

It was decades later before I'd have my own perilous experience with slicky pajamas, and it was all in an attempt to appreciate the efforts of my daughter and her three-year-old son, my grandson. I had traveled to spend some time with them in their home. They'd been busy making an etagere and small table for the guest room from a set of Omagles. Omagles are a not well known but remarkable building set for kids, a kind of giant Tinker Toy set with PVC pipes and connectors so that kid-sized tables, chairs, shelves, or even riding toys and more could be built. The table was colorful and was set with a nice tablecloth in hopes that visitors (such as me) could enjoy morning coffee there by the window in the guest room.

Several days had passed since I'd arrived, and my grandson asked me if I'd used the special table yet for my coffee. It made me sad to say, no, I had not yet used the pretty table, so I needed to remedy that.

One morning soon after that question, I made my coffee and took it upstairs to the special table. I had my coffee in a thermos to keep it warm, but had a nice mug to drink from. So, there I was, enjoying my coffee quietly at the special table until I heard stirrings in the rest of the house as the family began waking up. My daughter and grandson headed downstairs, and I gathered up my coffee mug in my left hand, and my coffee thermos in my right hand to head down as well to be sure my grandson could see that I'd had my coffee upstairs by the special table.

To get downstairs I had two sets of about six wooden stairs to navigate. First set down went fine, and I made the turn in my black slicky pajamas and my slick-bottomed house shoes to take the first step of the second set of stairs. It was at that moment of one misplaced step that I knew all was lost. I had no traction on the top step, my feet went out from under me, and, with absolutely no traction from my slicky pajamas or slicky housecoat to slow me down, I went down the stairs on my backside like a lugeless slider: kaboom, kaboom, kaboom, kaboom, kaboom, kaboom. Six kabooms later I was sitting silently on the foyer floor, stunned, my mug still in my left hand, and the only sound being my metal thermos pinging across the stone floor of the foyer. My daughter ran from a nearby room, she also silent, and I'm sure fearing she would find a limp GrandMaMa at the bottom of the stairs. My grandson called from another part of the house, "what happened?!"

I was saved serious injury by the grace of God and a well-padded backside that was ridiculously bruised but which served me well. The emotional trauma, however, was deep, and slicky pajamas have been added to my list of the literal pitfalls of growing older. I've known the hazards and have navigated throw rugs, power cords, and bathtub exits with extra care with each passing year. But, who knew slicky pajamas needed to be added to the list of hazards to both pride and body.

Consider yourself warned.

And my grandson definitely knows I had coffee upstairs at the special table.

Why I Wrote This

The lives of the families of my mother, growing and picking cotton in Alabama with her 6 sisters and 3 brothers, and my father, growing, cutting, and bunching tobacco, baling hay, and plowing behind a mule in Tennessee with his 1 sister and 4 brothers, have always held a fascination for me. Sadly, I never knew my maternal or paternal grandmothers. Both died before their children could know them fully, as well.

But in the tragedy and hardships, there were bonds built among them of beauty and talent, fashion and art, music and poetry. I heard stories from them that made me laugh and cry. I enjoy incorporating those stories in my writings where I can.

So, when I felt myself sliding down that staircase in my slick pajamas, my Aunt Dorothy telling this story of my Aunt Hazel sliding off the bed in her slick little negligee came to mind. What we'll do with the brute of a momma or grand-momma bear also came to mind. I believe that being present with those we love so that they will know our love and we will know their love is the greatest priority we can make.

October 25:
Sara McDaris

Sara McDaris served as storyteller for the Huntsville Public Library for many years. In this reading, she wonders. "what's going on?" Will her keen powers of observation help her figure it out?

What Was This All About?

Screaming! SCREAMing! SCREAMING!! Far, far away. As far as the free way. The screaming sound vibrated through the air, but I could also feel the intent: danger, coming your way; defend yourself; stay out of sight.

It was just after 10 PM when it started. And the shrillness of the sounds swelled. They were getting closer. I surmised that as many as three or four police cars were involved, each with its own clarion. Now they must be on one of the leading streets of the city, and growing ever closer. I listened for a crash to happen any second. I decided to turn off the light, knowing my doors were locked and thinking that an unknown person would be loose and could invade any available house.

Before I could move the screaming was closer than the usually busiest avenues near me: California south to north; Governor's Drive east to west. I was surprised to realize that the ever-penetrating screams were in my neighborhood, growing in volume with every breath I took. Then the sounds filled my street. Not only the clarion sounds, but a low growling, guttural sound of a car being forced to vault through the air at maximum speed. Its dark noise vied with the screams already on my street rushing toward the disappearing vehicle: a rich bass to be a ground for the shrill high sopranos.

The sounds enabled following the chase quite clearly, since I knew the neighboring streets. Whoever was driving the vehicle knew the area well. The car never turned on a dead-end street. Nor did it stop for a stop sign. Why was it taking so long for the chase cars to catch the fleeing car? Never did the volume of the clarion calls diminish. They circled and slowly their overwhelming vibrations lessened--only to begin expanding and growing again. Never having left the neighborhood, the chase continued, the escaping car traversing the same path: turning on my avenue, roaring forward with numbers of cars pressing closer toward it. The sounds of danger subsided, then once more grew as the lead car again turned on my street a half block away, but with the police's screaming sounds surrounding it.

It took me all of thirty seconds to hurry to the front door. The screaming had stopped. The lack of sound was as strong as the missing screams. I saw, three houses down, the flashing lights of the police cars filling up the street with others backing them up. The cul-de-sac just to the side of the blocking wall of light contained a single car with no lights on. I could see no movement, just occasionally a figure would pass in front of the cliff of lights, lights that I had never seen on a police car. They could have lit up a small town. No sounds. After a long wait, I saw the unlit car being backed up on to my street, moving toward my house, passing it, with a police car filing out of the side street only a house away. It followed the moving car.

Then I began to hear male voices full of excitement, relief, some laughter. The men of the light and the screaming were relaxing, again reliving the last twenty minutes: mission accomplished. No one hurt. I thought of the skillful driver of that car and how he/she now must be feeling. I thought about the men in blue, ready to pursue screams each time they left for work. And I wondered "What was this all about?"

November 1:
Kem Roper

I guess you could say I'm a certified nerd. I love books and coffee, God and family. I have a bachelor's degree in Communications, a Master's in English, and a PhD

in English Rhetoric and Composition. I currently direct a university writing center and have published my first book, a devotional for women called *Trust the Process: How Writing Can Help You Get Unstuck* on Amazon. I also host a weekly Facebook live broadcast called "Hey Girl!" that empowers and inspires women. I'm thankful every day for my daughters, who are my life and breath, and my husband who is the wind beneath my wings!

My Brief but Spectacular Take On...

Re-claiming creativity. "Adulting" is hard. When we're kids we're allowed—even encouraged—to have fun, to be creative! But as we grow older, we're expected to "put away childish things." Now we have to solve adult problems and there's no time for dallying with paint brushes and poetry.

So, we outgrow creativity. It falls by the wayside along with Santa Claus and the Easter Bunny, and the closer we get to adulthood, the more we learn that mistakes are to be avoided. Failure is not an option. We have to get it right the first time and we can't change our mind.

Seriously? I'd rather be a kid. What's great about kids is their knack for messing up and owning it. "Oops...sorry," they say, then dust themselves off and move on! Suppose you chose wrong—wrong job, wrong town, wrong path? Will you be an adult and explain it away, or be a kid and own it? "Oops...sorry!" Can you imagine yourself free—to move on, to explore, to be creative without apology? Let's re-claim our creativity—sorry, not sorry!

Keep Climbing!

They had no idea how afraid I was.

I could hear their voices down below, encouraging, cheerful—and their *laughter*! For them, this was all fun and games, but I was terrified! I wondered why I had agreed to do this. Why did I think I was up to the task? But I was stuck now. It was too late to turn back, yet I was uncertain of the way forward. I was in such a narrow spot and couldn't see the top from my vantage. My heart was pounding and I regretted keeping on the flannel-lined hoodie. The heat crept up my neck like mercury in a thermometer.

Then I heard his voice beside me. "Do you want to quit?"

In my mind I screamed "Yes!" But I couldn't bring myself to say so out loud.

"Come on, you can do it!" I heard them saying. Their confidence shocked me.

"You can do this." He added to their assurance with his own quiet push. "All you have to do is…"

Of course, "all I have to do is"—easy for him to say! Everything is easy for him! I'm the one who struggles. I'm the one who lacks confidence. Now here I am, on the brink of something, wavering and uncertain.

It's so typical of me.

Yet, to linger in that liminal space is always dangerous. While I waver, I give myself time to rehash all the reasons why I should quit. I recount all the things that are against me and all my weaknesses that make this present challenge impossible.

How many writers, or artists, start their masterpiece with great excitement, only to hit a wall and convince themselves that they aren't talented enough to complete it? How many projects have you started, then quit because it got too hard? And when you get to that point, how easy is it to get distracted by the success of others? "It's no use, we think to ourselves. Why did I ever think I could do this? How did I get here anyway?"

"Do you want to quit?"

"Yes!"

But, there's a crowd of people waiting for your book, your song, your poem, your *gift*—you can't quit now!

"You can do this" says the quiet voice right next to you. That soft, encouraging voice that you love. "You're stronger than you think and you're closer to the end than you realize."

No, it's not easy, but you've come too far to turn back—you might as well muster the strength to push forward.

That day on the sixty-foot climbing wall, I finally decided to push past my fear.

And when I did, something amazing happened. I pulled myself over the ledge! It had been just above me all along. The cheers of my supporters erupted all around and I had to fight back a little tear—I made it! My husband had climbed the wall with me and he gave me a high five. For me, it had been more than just a physical challenge. It was a mental challenge, symbolic of every mental battle I've ever fought.

Perhaps you need to hear this as much as I do: the success that you think is out of reach, is not. You just have to be brave enough to go for it. Your insecurities may be drowning out the assurances of loved ones, but you can decide to push past the fear. Move first and your mind will follow. Stop doubting and start believing that you ARE strong enough! It is at the point of your greatest despair when you will find that you are the closest to a turning point—if not the very summit that you've been seeking!

Just. keep. climbing.

Why I Wrote This

I wrote "Keep Climbing" for anyone who cares too much what people think. I'm especially writing to those of you who do creative work. Creators tend to be hated on. Who do you think you are? Get a real job! I'm often immobilized by these opinions. I have big dreams, but when I hold them up to the light of judgment or criticism, I'm defeated. I change my mind and stash those dreams away. That day on the climbing wall, my self-doubt was on full display, but something happened! Was it the adrenaline or physical exertion? I don't know, but I had an epiphany. With my husband by my side and my friends down below, I suddenly realized that everyone who mattered was *for me*. I wavered and considered turning back, but their voices spurred me on. It was encouragement, not judgment; confidence, not criticism. Suddenly my wall of doubt was surmountable!

It's easy to say "who cares what people think?" But the truth is, we all need someone in our corner. In the past I've allowed opinions to immobilize me, but that day I had a breakthrough. I was compelled to pull those dreams out, dust them off and try again.

© 2021 Kem Roper

November 8:
Rose Battle

I was born into a very large family. My father had nine siblings and my mother had seven. They married. We had an army of support growing up in the home our

father built for us in the woods on "Battle Hill" near Birmingham.

Our Battle family's life was centered on sports and politics. Our home life included our parents and the four of us children: Rose, Joe, Bill and Ginnie Battle, and our horse, monkey, dog and rooster.

All my life, I've written poems and stories for myself, and written and illustrated stories for the many

children in our family. I've told stories about "Battle Hill" in the 1940s and 1950s, as well as "Granny Stories" about our mother's mother. I do this to preserve our joys, our Southern ways, and words.

Nine years ago, I began appearing on WEUP Radio on *The 50 Yard Line*, a call-in sports show.

Thirteen years ago, I first tried out to be on WLRH Public Radio. I've loved telling my stories on the *Sundial Writers Corner*. It has led me to many opportunities to achieve my goal of sharing the great parts of growing up Southern.

My father would reply to any idea I had by saying, "Throw it out there, Sister Baby. Let's see if you have any takers."

So I have, and I am.

Trading in the Little Husband

Warning bells went off when Mother said we needed to do something about my hair before I started first grade. Mother, and Mother's 7 siblings, except Aunt Emily, had short hair. When I made my summer rounds to visit my Aunts, I felt my hair would be safe at Aunt Emily's home. Every morning Aunt Emily rolled up her knee-length hair on an oblong piece-of-thing-like foam. She made a large bun pinned onto the back of her head. She had hair! I felt safe.

Daddy drove me to Blountsville where Aunt Emily, Uncle Byron, our favorite cousin, Price, and George Pass lived, and ran the George Byron Pass General Mercantile Store, and lots of other things.

I was happy helping in the store, and playing with Price and his friends, until one day Aunt Emily said that Daddy called to tell her he wanted me to get my haircut and a "TON!" I could not believe that my daddy would try to make me go through all that getting "cutered up for nothing" as I called it. But, Aunt Emily said he did.

She sat me down on a pillow in a cane chair upstairs in their General Mercantile Store and proceeded to cut my long blonde hair up to almost the top of my ears! Then she got a "Toni" off the shelf and tortured me with curling rods and an awful smelling stuff called a "permanent."

When we walked home for lunch, I looked in their bedroom mirror and screamed! I was very small for my age, but my hair that was left was about 7 or 8 inches high straight up like a curly Vulcan way up in the air! I had no hair after you got to the top of my ears. I went out and hid at the cotton gin in their backyard.

When they came home for the evening, Uncle Byron, who was so dearly loved by everyone, came to find me. I told him I never wanted to go home again. He told me if I wanted to stay in Blountsville that he had a nice new hen house that he'd help me fix up. I could paint it any color I wanted to, and I figured Aunt Emily would make me flowerdy curtains from the gigantic flour sacks in their store. She made shortie pajamas of them for the 4 of us all the time.

Uncle Byron said he would get me a new washer and dryer, and a little husband about 6 or 7 years old. I could have my own home. So, I agreed to all that and began massive plans for my new life while wetting and batting down my culique hair tower up there over my ears. Before long, Daddy showed up, got out of the car, and I ran to hug him.

Daddy stopped and yelled, "Lord God, Sister Baby! What has happened to your hair?!" I didn't tell on Mother and Aunt Emily for their hair maneuver, but I did tell Daddy I could not leave my hen house, washer and dryer, or my little husband. Daddy sat down on the ground about then, and looked all done in.

I spent all the time I could when I was growing up watching Daddy doing political negotiations in back rooms. I sense it was time to start "The Wind Up, the Pitch, and the successful Resolution in My Favor" as

Daddy had taught me to do while watching him negotiate.

So, I said, "Daddy may I get some school supplies for first grade that I really need that some others might not think I need?"

He said, "What would those supplies be?"

I said, "Red shoes with taps on the heels and toes, and a little red purse to hold my new "Paint the Town Red" Lipstick.

He said, "That sounds mighty fine to me! How about we go thank Aunt Emily and Uncle Byron and head on home to Battle Hill then, Sister Baby?"

I could tell Daddy still looked alarmed when he looked at my Vulcan statue of curls up over my ears, but he was adjusting fairly well in a short period of time. So, I waved goodbye to my Blountsville kin, I hugged Price goodbye, told my little hen house, my future washer and dryer, my long hair, and my little husband all goodbye.

A week later, I tap danced down the bright hall of my new school swinging my new red purse with my lips slathered to high heavens in my school supply of "Paint the Town Red" lipstick. My Toni curls piled high having successfully negotiated away my little husband for school supplies – now on my way to a successfully negotiated happy education!

© 2021 Rose Battle

November 15:
Monita Soni

With one foot in Huntsville, the other in India and a heart steeped in humanity, writing is a contemplative practice. Borrowing a tweet from a red cardinal, the wind whistling through green meadows, a child's laughter, a twinkle from fireflies, I weave poems. Nature has given me an outline of my own masterpiece. I delight in writing and coloring on my notepad. I write, rewrite and write some more. The more I write, the more I fall in love with the craft. The stories I hear, read and recount embody me...Like old friends, bedazzled with the blessings.

My Brief but Spectacular Take On...

My favorite drink is a glass of milk. Growing up, I drank milk all the time. It was milk if I was hungry, angry, or tired. In the morning, I had a cup of steaming fresh milk with tasty toast. In the evening, it was cold chocolate milk. At night, it was milk infused with cardamom, almonds, and saffron to induce good sleep. Milk with home-made cookies was always a good pick-me-up snack. I started drinking tea in the early 1990s when I worked at the Cancer Clinic at Tata Memorial Hospital, in Bombay. Other interns used to gather for tea in the morning while reviewing cases. Once in a while, my dad encouraged me to try a cup of tea with him. Dad had bed tea in the morning. I was very amused by him trying to drink tea while lying on his side. It was my task to make sure he was alert enough to drink it and did not spill it all over himself. In the US, I drink more coffee than tea but when I go to India, I favor Indian chai. In the last few years, my mother's nurse, Bindu, would make tea for her in the morning. At home, we got fresh milk every day at about seven AM. Most of it is used up during the day. Bindu would save half a cup of milk in the refrigerator for the 6 AM morning *chai*. When I visited, I would be up before dawn and in my mother's room. My mother wanted me to share tea with her but Bindu had milk only for two cups so she blatantly ignored me. My sweet mother would "cut" her *chai* with me. While Bindu sipped her full cuppa without blinking an eye.

Cutting Chai Anyone?

It's October again. It's fall weather. Time to sit on porch swings with families. A dog and a cat, a talking parrot, a goldfish. Enjoy the colorful foliage. The pandemic has brought us outdoors. People are sipping pumpkin spice lattes. If you visit me, I may treat you to a special drink from my mother's kitchen. Cutting chai. What is cutting chai? If you are a fan of ice tea but are not afraid to try hot tea, cha*i* tea, you might want to learn about "cutting chai". Teatime was sacred at our home. Water boiled in a whistling kettle, and transferred with tea leaves into a Dresden China tea kettle. Kept warm with a hand embroidered tea-cosy and served with a plate of assorted cookies, a must on every tea tray. My daughter loved to raid my mom's cookie tin and steal her orange cream biscuits and chocolate bonbons before anyone else got their sticky fingers on them. When we moved to Mumbai, we adopted the tradition of cutting chai. At the crack of dawn, my mom would boil one cup of water in a saucepan, add half a teaspoon of grated fresh ginger, and stir in two crushed pods of fragrant cardamom. Once the water started boiling, she would add one heaped spoon of Darjeeling tea. Slowly she would pour half a cup of creamy milk and let it mingle. She would bring the chai to a boil for a whole minute, letting it swell up to the brim, but not overflow. Then, at a predetermined magical moment just lower the heat. She chanted vedic hymns and let the scriptures simmer in with the gently plumped tea leaves. Swishing and swirling the bisque, pink aromatic liquid, ever so gently. With love and care. The first cup of chai was always important. It was life enhancing. It was her only cup of tea. As she made tea, the tea leaves whispered back to her. Told her stories of the lush tea estates, set in the panoramic Himalayan foothills and bewitching Nigir*i* mountains.

Mom is very traditional. She has one favorite brand, Brooke Bond Red label loose tea. Her cup of tea tastes the same every time she makes it. It has a comfort of familiarity. A rhythm of continuity. Sustenance. But my sister has an eclectic tea collection: Butter teas, Kashmir kahwas, Assam teas, Noon chais, White jasmine teas and white tip teas from the Doddabetta biosphere on the western ghats of India. I love my sister's lemon grass tea but still yearn for Mom's *chai* with a dollop of honey in it. When I visit Bombay, I make chai sometimes. Or I enter the kitchen on cue to pick up the saucepan and drain the tea into small terracotta tapris or tiny glasses suitable for "cutting chai". This term is very common among Mumbaikar*s*. They cut their chai. I often wondered how they did it? Did they cut the tea leaves with a special instrument? Or was the flamboyant stream of chai cut while being poured ever so delicately into a cup? But this is not the case. Chai is liquid, and liquid can't be cut. Simple rules of physics! It's common Indian courtesy to offer guests/ clients chai when they come to your home or place of business. It's customary. It is also considered rude to refuse chai. It is a double whammy.

Cutting chai was invented by merchants in Mumbai who became over-caffeinated by drinking several cups of tea during the day. So they came up with a system of cutting the tea by half. They divided the tea and only had half a cup. Offered the other half to a friend. But since then, it has become fashionable to order "cutting chai". You can get "cutting chai" at cafes or tea stalls. It's like a small espresso cup and gives a quick "pick-me-up" in a few sips at half the price. So it serves the purpose and also does not *cut* into your budget or cut your stomach. Another fun fact about Mumbai is that people are always on the go. They have to travel long distances, change buses and trains. So they don't have time to linger. I think it is very good that the tradition has been adopted by one and all. You can order "cutting chai" in fancy restaurants and they proudly serve it in the traditional glasses. You can buy a set of six with a metal carrier like the ones used by street vendors on Etsy, Amazon, Pottery Barn. Isn't it amazing? But perhaps you would like to travel with me to the hometown of this signature chai? I am keeping my fingers crossed that this Christmas, I will be able to "cut" chai with my sweet mom and share one of her favorite cookies.

Why I Wrote This

Morning prayer and morning tea with my mother conjure poignant memories for me. In the last decade, I flew to India at least once a year to check on mom. Her health was frail and her energy limited. After night's sleep, and morning sponging, she was well-rested, so I made it a point to share tea with her. It was very pleasant to be in her serene company, her loving gaze upon me. I have not been able to travel like so many of us in the last two years, as COVID cases rose, plateaued and rose again. A few months back, India was in the deathly grip of the highly contagious variant. My mother was not vaccinated. India was closed to international visitors. It was a nightmare! In October, when I wrote this piece, there was a sense of optimism. Vaccines were working. The COVID spike had ebbed. So one morning, as I made a cup of tea for myself, I thought about "cutting chai" In India. I booked my tickets and hoped to sip a fragrant cup of tea with her. But my mother went into atrial fibrillation on the 22nd of October and passed away on the evening of the 30th. I was there to share a final prayer in the hospital room at MGM hospital but could never share "chai" with her.

November 22:
Sam Mitchell

Graphic designer and illustrator Sam Mitchell (he/him/his) is now located in Huntsville, Alabama.  When he's is not binging Netflix, listening to Hall & Oates, or obsessing over his toy collection, he also likes to tell stories. Sam is host and co-founder of *Tin Can Stories* and a proud member of *Out Loud HSV*. He has been featured at *Write Club ATL*, *Tenx9 Nashville*, the Princess Theater: Center for Performing Arts, and on the *Sundial Writers Corner*. His work can be viewed at blood-sweatandtype.com.

Misconceptions and the High-Waisted Mermaid

As a child, it's sometimes hard to imagine what some people looked like when they were young. In the autumn of her life, Louise Bevel had short, dark gray, curly hair, sported high waisted slacks and rarely wore a smile. Even though she was of average size, she gave the appearance of someone much larger and more broad-shouldered. She was no nonsense country, whereas her best friend, Margaret, was petite and a bit refined.

You see Margaret was my grandmother. She had been a teacher, been married to a lawyer and played piano for her church, but Louise was the epitome of rough. She wasn't prone to much dialogue and when she did speak, her collective amount of words didn't add to much. She would most often grumble an "hmm, mmm" in response to someone else. This was the picture of Louise that most people knew.

Even in her eulogy, the minister couldn't paint the softest of images, he said that anyone who knew her would say she was gruff. But despite her gruffness, Louise could be tender, but only as tender as Louise could be. On occasion, she would baby sit me when my grandmother could not. One time I remember looking up at her and saying "Ouise, I love ooo, do ooo love me?"

And instead responding like most people by saying, "Of course Sam, I love you", she looked down, and in her brusque fashion said, "Sam, everyone loves ooo."

***

Coincidentally, my grandmother and Louise both had lost their husbands in their thirties. My grandfather, Roy, was killed when a train ran into his truck as he was coming back from his family's dairy farm and Louise's husband had had a heart attack. Neither remarried. When my grandmother was asked why she never married again, she would always say that she could never replace the best. When Louise was asked the same question, I imagine her response might have been, "What Margaret said."

Instead of remarrying, they chose to remain single and used each other for companionship. This included vacations, dinners, and of course, trips to the movies.

Before Rotten Tomatoes, I would get short summations from them about what movie they had seen the night before at our small one screener, The Ritz. Reviews were always mixed, but one movie that they both agreed they liked was Ron Howard's 1984 comedy, *Splash*.

For those of you too young to remember, *Splash* was the story of Allen Bauer, played by Tom Hanks, a produce business owner in New York and how he finds his soulmate, but she just happens to be a real-life mermaid. The movie begins with a sepia toned flashback where an eight-year old Hanks instinctively jumps off a small sight-seeing boat off the coast of Cape Cod even though he cannot swim. He sees a blonde girl of the same age in the ocean and realizes that with her he can now breathe underwater. Hanks is quickly pulled back to the surface, and as an adult he believes his experience with the young mermaid to be a hallucination.

When *Splash* came to home-video I was about 7. If you believe my embarrassing misconception about the movie was that I thought mermaids were real, then you'd be dead wrong. But I was in awe of how innovative and lucky the filmmakers were to have started filming the movie twenty years prior to capture the flashback scene between Hanks and Darryl Hannah when they were only kids. It never even occurred to me that the director had hired two different actors to play the same character.

***

My greater misconception was that Grandma and Louise were just two old women whose lives were compartmentalized to enjoying movies, cruises and food, but companionship is nothing without a little adventure. Evident of their deep friendship was the fact that Louise would ride around with my grandmother forcing their way into other people's business. Perhaps inspired by Grandma's love for Harlequin Romances mixed with an unhealthy amount of soaps and *Divorce Court*, they both became sleuths. An outsider would have called them busybodies, but since it's my own grandma, I'll say that she and Louise were amateur extra-marital detectives. On a whim, Grandma and Louise would chariot around a rumored victim in an affair and stalk the two-timing husband and try to catch him in the act. Sometimes this would take weeks. Many times, they would give the aggrieved wife the evidence and/or the courage that she needed to move on with her life.

I can imagine my grandma, binoculars around her neck, behind the steering wheel, moving through rural Georgia. Louise is in the passenger seat, lit cigarette in her mouth, taking notes and occasionally grumbling, "What a bastard," while a bewildered wife looks on wildly from the backseat of Grandma's green Chevy Nova, wondering what in the ever-living hell had she gotten herself into.

***

When she turned 80, my grandmother was admitted to Providence Care Nursing home. After a year at her new residence something peculiar happened. My dad went by for his daily visit with her and what he found was not the cheerful mother that he usually saw; the one who was either reading her Harlequins or watching the Braves game. Grandma was slumped over in her bed, sobbing into her pillow.

"Mama, what is it? What's wrong?", he said.

"Oh, Louise!", Grandma said. "Louise is dead!"

My father assured her that Louise was very much alive.

Maybe it was a premonition by someone who was so connected to another person, but the next day Louise did indeed die. My grandmother was heartbroken.

Two years later, my grandmother died from her own heart failure.

***

Soulmate doesn't always mean the person that you've fallen in love with. Sometimes a soul mate is the person who you've grown with the most. Soulmates can be forged by experience. And I truly believe that Grandma and Louise were partners in crime, partners in life, and were most assuredly soulmates.

For my grandmother, if heaven exists, I imagine it in sepia tones and instead of pearly gates, I see her being ferried to heaven in a small tour boat. She has been transformed to a young girl of eight. She looks out in the water and sees another young girl with short dark curls, swimming freely in the water, a high-waisted mermaid. It's Louise. Grandma jumps in, they swim toward each other, they clasp one another's hands and my grandmother can breathe once again.

© 2021 Sam Mitchell

November 29:
Sri Bhooshanan

Sri Bhooshanan is a long-time resident of Madison, AL, and lives with his wife and 3 daughters, one of whom has four legs. He's a software engineer, and

fancies himself a word engineer, aka writer.

He is passionate about music, reading, traveling, attending concerts, and eating right most of the time. He is grateful to WLRH and the Madison Public Library as formative forces in his American life. He is happy to be alive in America and is yet nostalgic about his salad days in Bombay, where he was enveloped by his family's love, graced by his teachers at St. Xavier's High School and College, and first savored the delicate notes of rock n roll and ragda patties.

My Brief but Spectacular Take On...

Being Izzy. When our kids were young, I enjoyed looking at the world through their eyes — their innocence, their insatiable curiosity, and their infectious belly laughs! They have since "growed up." Enter Izzy — our 12-pound bichon frisé — who fell fortuitously into our lap. I now enjoy seeing the world through her eyes and incorporating some of her traits. She might as well have written the book, *How To Win Friends And Influence People.* When one sees that bundle of fluff come up, lie on her back with paws folded, begging for a belly rub, one capitulates with a smile and proceeds to deliver that belly rub. She's as gentle with babies (Hi Zelli!) as she is with near centenarians (Hi Nana!) In my book she can do no wrong. Izzy always strikes a yoga pose when she awakes from a nap. Now I try to get some exercise soon after I wake up. She only wants the basics - food, shelter, and a whole lot of love in between. Who wouldn't want that? She has an uncanny knack of adapting to situations and has a sunny outlook on life — traits we'd do well to emulate during a pandemic or otherwise. I will miss her when she is gone. In the meantime, I will be as generous with my belly rubs as Izzy is with her lick baths.

Killer Queen

Late one evening during the early days of the pandemic, I let Izzy out into our backyard. Izzy is our sweet-natured 12-pound bichon, who had been with us about 9 months. Her life's aphorism is: "A stranger is a friend I've never met." She is loved by one and all who meet her and has the gentlest personality. She is as gentle around babies as she is around near centenarians.

That evening, Izzy went sniffing around our vegetable garden. Suddenly, a rabbit jumped out of the darkness and started hopping away. Izzy gave chase, but its hops quickly widened the distance between them. Then, I noticed a baby rabbit, with its short hops, trying to catch up to mama. Izzy's killer instinct kicked in and she pounced on the poor baby bunny. My initial reaction was to curse and ask Izzy to stop. This was no way to raise our dog – being a bully and picking on someone much smaller. This was uncharted territory. The closest we've seen her killer instinct was when she played with her stuffed toy pig, which she would toss up in the air and pounce upon, as it makes a squeaky sound.

Unlike Izzy's toy pig which lay quite still when she pounced on it, this little bunny would jump away. I reconciled to let nature take its course. It was a heartbreaking sight. Izzy would pounce on the baby bunny, bite it, and step back. The baby bunny would squeal in pain and stand still. As soon as it managed a feeble hop, Izzy would pounce on it, and this cycle would repeat. The screams would intensify progressively, which was almost deafening, in the still of the night. I was reminded of the scene in *The Silence of the Lambs*, where Dr. Lecter asks the ingenue FBI agent, "Well, Clarice, have the lambs stopped screaming?"

I watched and wondered if it were right for me to quell Izzy's instinct that had been honed over thousands of years. A few minutes later, the bunny fell silent. Izzy now started to eat her kill. Dear Izzy, who would reluctantly eat her kibbles and boiled chicken, was savoring haute cuisine in a most savage way. I moved toward Izzy, who immediately snatched the bunny in her jaws, and ran toward the back porch, with me in hot pursuit. When she got to the bottom of the deck stairs, she dropped the bunny. I scooped Izzy up, slid the storm door open and called out to my wife. I quickly described what had happened. Parvathy brought out some plastic bags for me, and took Izzy to the garage, for an "express wash".

I went back to the yard to see the late baby bunny, with its head facing me, and its legs up in the air, quite still. Yes, Dr. Lecter, this bunny had stopped screaming. I turned the bag inside out, and triple bagged the bunny, which felt quite soft through the plastic. I disposed of it immediately. Meanwhile, Izzy had returned and was standing by the storm door, eager to go off and play with her new toy or scarf it down. I let her back onto the deck, and Izzy dashed to the bottom of the stairs, to find … nothing. She sniffed around frantically for any remains. She began retracing her steps all the way back to the scene of the crime, and still found nothing. Obviously miffed, and after sniffing around some more, Izzy made her way back into the house.

Izzy and mama bunny taught me a couple of life lessons that night: First, it's a jungle out there; Second, stay fit, as you never know when you might need to hightail it out of a situation.

I shared a sanitized version of the incident with our daughters, who got upset. We soon settled in for the night, each one of us a little shaken by what our sweet natured Izzy had morphed into — a killer queen.

Why I Wrote This

This incident, which took place in the early days of the pandemic, formed an impression on me. I have always been moved by nature documentaries of predators eating their kill as they go about their grazing. Izzy had been with us about 9 months, and we had only seen her gentle side. Even this incident did not make her a bad dog - just incongruent with the image the Bhooshanans had created of her – which was mea culpa. We tend to project our humanness onto our pets and forget that they are descendants of wild ancestry with sharpened survival instincts. Another thought that came to mind was how parents facing danger in some form would generally fight back to stave off a predator, and save the child, but mama bunny's only thought was her own survival so she could make more babies at a future time. That law of the jungle was brought home in a most vivid way that early spring night.

I also enjoy intertwining movies, music, and mirth in my musings. *Silence of the Lambs"* is one of my favorite movies (apologies to Sir Hopkins and Ms. Foster for my ersatz impression of Dr. Lecter and Agent Starling; Dorrie Nutt of WLRH was able to "score" the piece with a tease of "Goodbye Horses" at the start and close with Queen's "Killer Queen."

And mirth??? As Meatloaf sings, "Two out of three ain't bad!"

December 6:
Patricia Sammon

I was born and raised in Canada, studied history and philosophy at Cornell and then Queen's University, and have been lucky enough to call the magnificent

 Tennessee Valley home for forty years. Through the decades, the fact that Judy and Harry Watters were expecting another Sundial essay provided the most welcome nudge to pay attention to the world around me, whether I was kayaking at Wheeler or pushing a swing at a playground. The invitation to compose some thoughts on a topic heightened my awareness of the splendor and humor and poignancy of my ordinary days. And for this I am forever grateful.

Magic Shows

A while ago we invited a magician into our living room to entertain the kids of the neighborhood. With long-fingered ease he'd demonstrate yet again that there was nothing in his hand, which meant of course, suddenly and unaccountably there *was* something in his hand: the missing red scarf, a stack of silver coins, a squeeze flower that issued its own shower of water droplets. The children watched wide-eyed, utterly enthralled. The parents fell under the spell of their own children and gloried in such innocence, such eagerness. At the end of the show the visitors filed out the front door, back into the ordinary world where things rarely appear just because you've reached into thin air for them. Our older son, seven at the time, watched the magician pack up his gear, fold up the little table, close up the briefcase, collapse the top hat and stash the white gloves.

By way of talking shop for a few minutes, the magician said, "Yeah, I'm thinking about adding a trick with a guinea pig." To which our son countered, "Guinea pigs are really kind of boring. They just sit there. You should have a trick with something exciting, like a Gila monster or a giraffe."

The magician, not realizing this particular magic show was far from over, said, "Yeah, well, you see, I don't own a Gila monster or a giraffe. What I've got is a guinea pig."

From the young face came a look of such withering puzzlement. "You're a magician." Which was to say,

"Get a grip, man. Remember who you are. We're not talking about a trip to a pet store. Just say 'Giraffe!' — and stand back."

In the scientific world there are no abracadabra moments, and there are lots of guinea pigs. Rigorous, methodical inquiry is very much the opposite of *tah-dah*-style magic. But think of Louis Pasteur in his top hat walking through a hospital ward, waving his empty hand through the empty air and saying, "It only looks like there's nothing in my hand, but there are microscopic organisms floating about, and there are germs causing these infections all around us."

Or think of Wilhelm Röentgen who deduced the existence of invisible radiation. He even used them to take an X-ray photograph of his wife's hand, revealing not the white gloves fashionable in 1895, but a fan of tiny bones beneath the skin and muscles.

Or think of atomic physicist, Wolfgang Pauli, puzzling over the odd angles by which beta particles decay. Instead of shrugging off the weirdness as an artifact, he predicted the existence of a ghostly subatomic particle. He said it would have almost no mass and absolutely no electrical charge. Magician-like, Pauli managed to look into the nothingness and forecast the existence of a vanishingly small 'something'. That proposed 'something' was eventually discovered and named the neutrino. Neutrinos are so infinitesimally small they can pass directly through a whole stack of silver coins. Pauli said we should picture them as a spray of water droplets that are drenching us day and night. And isn't that the idea with science — that very often, "Nothing up my sleeve," means something amazing in my open hand.

And isn't that the idea with science — that very often, "Nothing up my sleeve," means something amazing in my open hand.

December 13:
Brad Posey

Brad Posey lives in Ardmore with his wife, kids, dogs, and chickens. When he's not working on his next episode of "The Invisible City," he's pursuing his passions for music and visual arts.

The Cannibal Pygmies of Hazel Green, Alabama

Blown out summers
With my redneck cousins
Dust sparks floating
Through the living room
Like stars in the night sky
Bleeding and popping
Across the screen
Like old film footage
Our dirty faces stalking
Through the corn
Emerging from the jungle
Hunting for crusaders
To fill our bellies
Eons away from hollow institutions
Like school, church, country or government
Far removed from dead concepts
Like bed times or haircuts
Or the prison of the clock
Free as beasts, our bodies
Our hands painted with mud
We tore through the backyard
On countless suicide missions
And lived to tell the tale
We rode bikes on wet streets
Played space ship in junked out cars
Our best friends were dogs
We took turns standing in the bucket
Full of air conditioner water
As holy as the Ganges

We swore allegiance only to each other
And the next moment
I miss the ghosts of those boys
Those memories that walk the earth
No monuments now, no parades
Maybe just this, for those
Long ago days.
Somehow I walked through
The museum of time
My little bones free of disease
My brown eyes clear
No hands ever poisoned me
No chains held me
I dreamed I was a bird
On a thousand summer days
Bounding from ground to cloud
To branch to blue
All my random movements
In some unknown pattern
All corresponding lines
On some unseen map of the heavens
Woven, electric, a splatter of stars
Maybe God never took his hands
Off me, maybe I am guided still
Maybe every minute of every experience
Sewn and deliberate
Each time I fell and skint my knees
I got up and ran like a deer through the trees
Only coaxed indoors for a cookie
Or a slice of bologna or a Mountain Dew.
After storms we would swim

In the ditch, jump and shout
At passing cars like feral cavemen
Fresh from a time warp
Fresh from the bog
Brought to the present
Resurrected from the Primordial
Blinking, yawping
Shaking spears
Where was National Geographic
To take our picture
Where was some brave mad
Explorer to witness
The cannibal pygmies
Of Hazel Green, Alabama.

© 2021 Brad Posey

December 20:
Cathie Mayne

Since moving to Huntsville in 2002, I've had the honor of promoting the missions of three unique local nonprofits: the Land Trust of North Alabama, the

 Catalyst Center for Business & Entrepreneurship, and the Huntsville – Madison County Senior Center. During my career as a public relations and nonprofit management professional, I've won some awards along the way, planned memorable special events, developed an extensive contact network, and strengthened fund development.

Following my retirement from the Land Trust, WLRH Station Manager Brett Tannehill kindly let me wield the community microphone for the fledgling *Public Radio Hour*. One of my interviews helped the station win a state award and that was such a proud moment!

My Brief but Spectacular Take On...

Acceptance. I've always affirmed, "I'm a dog person." Other family members are considered cat whisperers. When we took in two cats following the death of a friend, I knew they'd eventually be the familiars of someone else.

The older feline gentleman took the longest to accept our family. He found all the best places to hide and sulk. I fed, watered, and scooped for both of them, but wasn't his favorite.

Now I understand cats scratch to mark territory. Shredded couch upholstery proves this. What I did not know was the power of being chosen and claimed by the simple touch of a cat.

As I sat in front of my computer, the elderly cat startled me by jumping onto the desk. He padded slowly over papers and past an empty wine glass. Unbidden, he lay his thin body in front of the keyboard and placed a paw firmly on my left wrist. And, he pressed down as if his paw were a stamp. Essentially holding me in place, he gave two owl-like blinks and lowered his head to sleep.

Immobilized, I felt truly accepted and claimed. Verklempt and work forgotten, I let him sleep for a very, very long time.

The Earnest Little Angel

Many years ago I was thrilled to be cast as the angel in my church Christmas morning service. As I donned my gold tinsel halo and white cotton robe, I was determined to be the most reverent and awe-inspiring angel ever.

When the Presbyterian congregation began singing the first carol, I slowly raised my hands in gracious benediction over the manger and lifted my face in praise to the heavens (er, ceiling) above.

My dramatic pose lasted just short of two verses and I slowly lowered my arms to regain circulation. Hoping that no one noticed my lapse of reverence, I raised my arms again...held them...then lowered them inch by inch. For an hour, our tableau had an angel that looked as if she were flying in slow motion.

The drama of the little nativity was simply too great for one of the five-year-old sheep. He saw his family in the pews and quickly toddled offstage. One of the wise men locked his knees and gently sank to the floor in a faint. Another wise man decided that kneeling for an hour was unbearable, so she sat cross-legged for the latter half of the service. The shepherd watched the crook of his staff lazily go back and forth like a metronome. Little Mary sat on a small stool and nodded in sleep. And my angel just kept flying.

Adults hid their laughter and afterwards solemnly pronounced the service a success. However, two performances were given that morning - the first and the last time that children under the age of twelve were asked to remain in "Live Nativity" mode for an entire worship service.

I sometimes think of that earnest little angel when I reach "life during the holidays" overload. She helps me remember that it's not my efforts to make things "just right" that matter most. For if we try too hard to keep our wings - and drama - in motion, we may miss the small, comforting, much more important Presence in the manger.

Why I Wrote This

Ah, downsizing. A universal cause of reminiscing.

My growing pile of empty plastic tubs confirms that my current downsizing efforts are being successful. It's slow going when I come across fun memories like a little angel from college that makes me laugh and I then think about my late momma.

Angels and arrows are the symbols of my beloved college women's fraternity. It's always tickled me that my momma gave me one of the first in my angel collection. Perhaps it was simply the first angel she found in a card store after I pledged, but the little American Greetings statuette is a chubby 70's styled creature with eyes demurely closed and hands folded devoutly in prayer. The incongruous wording on the base, however, reads "Do Thine Own Thing."

My Christmas pageant story features a much younger me, but maybe Momma remembered that earnest little "flying" angel when she purchased this sassy plastic piece for her collegiate daughter.

Do Thine Own Thing girl now rests next to a tall angel sculpture with dramatic flowing robes and classic wings. They represent two very different times in my life. Nevertheless, I like to think that they are the very best of friends.

© 2021 Cathie M Mayne

December 27:
Kathryn Tucker Windham

For Kathryn Tucker Windham, our planet's oral sto-
rytelling tradition is an important historical record.
She challenged us to preserve that record by

remembering and retelling old stories of our family,
friends and communities ... like the Tale of the Rev-
erend Smalls, which lives on through the dozens of
yellow Lady Banks rose cuttings that still bloom in
gardens and landscapes around downtown Selma, Al-

abama. This story is a transcription of Mrs. Windham's retelling of the Tale of the Reverend Smalls, and appears with permission from her family. *(Mrs. Windham passed away on June 12, 2011. Her biography is shared by Brett Tannehill)*

The Legend of Reverend Arthur Smalls

Flower lovers in Selma look forward to the Spring when the Lady Bankshire roses bloom all over the city. And nearly every rose bush thats make those yellow roses came from a single plant at the Presbyterian Church that has a history that is closely associated with the history of Selma.

It was the spring of 1865 in April, that the Battle of Selma was fought. Nearly the end of that war, that war that divided this country. The South was on its last gasp almost, and the Yankee troops were riding in to take Selma. It was on a Sunday morning, and the call went out for every able-bodied man to report to the trenches around Selma to help protect the city.

At the Presbyterian Church, the minister, a young man 33-years old, the Reverend Arthur Smalls was in the church getting ready to deliver his Sunday message. I don't know who he expected to have in the congregation that Sunday. But he heard the call to help protect the city, and he left the pulpit and went out to try and do what he could for a city he loved. And he was killed in the Battle of Selma. And they say they brought that young man's battered body back to the Presbyterian manse.

There was a Lady Bankshire rose that grew over the entranceway of the house where they brought the body. It was in full bloom. And they say when they brought that young man's body up the front steps and toward the front door that the rose bush shed its golden petals like tears on his body. And that story has been repeated year after year after year after year. And that rose bush that wept on the body of that young Presbyterian minister still blooms every spring by the Presbyterian Church in Selma. And all over Selma, there are bushes that are cuttings from the bush that shed their tears on the Reverend Smalls.

Bonus: A Sundial Christmas

Not satisfied with providing us with 52 weeks of Sundial sun through the year, Brett and Dorrie gathered seven favorite stories together for a special Sundial reading to celebrate Christmas.

Reverie

by Rosemary McMahan

The tree stands bare in the spill
of white candlelight
that beckons remembrance,
the still air laden with pungent pine.
I unwrap memories
lifted from silk-worn boxes,
and passing years emerge,
reflecting faces mirrored
in each round and shiny ball.

A piece of crumpled tissue drops
and here is the rocking horse
suspended on a crimson string
that marked my son's first outing,
creamed soup with his aunties,
when he was three. And here,
the fading Polaroid photo
of my daughter's smiling face
pasted in the middle of a holiday bell,
the sparkling glitter reminiscent
of her five-year old's laughter.

An angel carved from sea shell
reminds me of my once best-
friend, now divorced
and distanced. We birthed our
daughters the same month.

A cross-stitched cherubim
handmade by a companion
along the way who died
too young takes center place
near the top of the tree.
A widowed neighbor designed
the snowman decked in felt,
with his black pipe,
for each of my mother's
daughters some forty years ago,
and the sweetgum ball covered
in tin foil by the hands of
my husband's father, gone
ten years, is a mirror
of his own Christmases past.

Like rainbow-hued lights,
heart-rooted presence is wound
about fragrant branches
that fill the room
reaching to the ceiling
evidence of the many incarnations
I have lived--
precious as the first brush
of silent snow.

© Rosemary McMahan

All the Ugly Ornaments
by Melissa Ford Thornton

October's arrival in the South is bittersweet for me. Like the grass beneath my feet, I'm reluctant to let go of the memory of summer's warmth. Evenings are filled with nostalgic scents of wood smoke and the musty tang of leaves grown brittle and weary as an old man's sigh. Most of my friends grow excited thinking ahead to the holidays. But my mind travels back in time even as I begin to peruse holiday cards and deliberately select a misshapen pumpkin.

You see, the holidays of my childhood weren't the stuff of Pinterest – those symmetrical trees and elaborate mantel displays. Rather, they were filled with the messy stuff of glue and glitter and homemade Toll House cookies – always a bit burnt on the bottom from mom's thin cookie sheets.

My brothers and their friends filled the house with rock music that clashed with Dad's vinyl collection of Christmas songs sung in Spanish, reminiscent of his native Mexico. Mom always insisted on a real tree – the more lopsided and sad-looking, the better. She was tender-hearted that way, never wanting to see something or someone left lonely or unwanted.

Decorating was an adventure. We'd lug dusty boxes from the attic and untangle moldy popcorn strings from ornaments with the names of pets who'd crossed over the rainbow bridge years before I was born. I'd hear the tales of "Skippy – the best dog

EVER" as we strung tinsel that sparked and clung to us with static.

And there were more ugly ornaments. Most crafted by hands not gifted with talent or any sense of aesthetic: like popsicle-stick elves my brothers and I made with frightening googly eyes; paper plates filled with plaster of Paris imprinted with our tiny hands and painted to look like turkeys or angels – it was hard to tell which. Mom lovingly hung every single one – on the *back* of the tree.

Our favorite ugly ornament was strangely oversized and fragile. Every year when Mom handed this pink ornament to me, memory transported me to the day she allowed each of us kids to select one decoration from a specialty shop on the square. It was a beautiful place. Brightly colored spools of Tartan ribbon spilled into the aisles, perfectly-shaped artificial trees twinkled with fairy lights, and Christmas carols drifted from speakers. Unlike at home, lyrics to Silver Bells and Frosty the Snowman were sung in English.

We took our time making our selections. My brothers each came away with a glass-blown, delicate creation that brought a smile and nod of approval from the shop owner – a toy soldier, Santa, a sleigh. Then they all turned to see what I, the youngest child, had chosen. A ballerina from the Nutcracker, perhaps? But no, here was an animal of unrecognizable species. The bewhiskered nose and paws indicated a mouse. The curly tail and distinctive hog-shaped ears made us lean toward a pig. The proprietor rang up the sale – with a discount.

Mom smiled and shrugged. No accounting for a child's taste. And each year we carefully added Pig-Mouse to our Charlie Brown tree's branches.

Today, as I kicked through leaves trying to unbury patches of green grass on my morning run, I thought of the way October ushered in holidays so slowly as a child and how quickly now those days speed towards us once pumpkins appear on doorsteps.

Soon, it'll be time for me to pull dusty boxes from the attic; boxes that hold plaster of Paris thumb prints that our son made nearly two decades ago. And when I, like my mom before me, place those near the back of the tree, I recognize that's a place of honor. Not facing our small living room, but rather displaying them in the window for neighbors and friends and all who come to call to admire. Truly my mother's daughter, I find the things that decorate our hearts, all the ugly ornaments that make up perfectly imperfect lives, precious and timeless.

© Melissa Ford Thornton

The Earnest Little Angel
by Cathie Mayne

Many years ago I was thrilled to be cast as the angel in my church Christmas morning service. As I donned my gold tinsel halo and white cotton robe, I was determined to be the most reverent and awe-inspiring angel ever.

When the Presbyterian congregation began singing the first carol, I slowly raised my hands in gracious benediction over the manger and lifted my face in praise to the heavens (er, ceiling) above.

My dramatic pose lasted just short of two verses and I slowly lowered my arms to regain circulation. Hoping that no one noticed my lapse of reverence, I raised my arms again...held them...then lowered them inch by inch. For an hour, our tableau had an angel that looked as if she were flying in slow motion.

The drama of the little nativity was simply too great for one of the five-year-old sheep. He saw his family in the pews and quickly toddled offstage. One of the wise men locked his knees and gently sank to the floor in a faint. Another wise man decided that kneeling for an hour was unbearable so she sat cross-legged for the latter half of the service. The shepherd watched the crook of his staff lazily go back and forth like a metronome. Little Mary sat on a small stool and nodded in sleep. And my angel just kept flying.

Adults hid their laughter afterwards and solemnly pronounced the service a success. However, two performances were given that morning - the first and the last time that children under the age of twelve were asked to remain in "Live Nativity" mode for an entire worship service.

I sometimes think of that earnest little angel when I reach "life during the holidays" overload. She helps me remember that it's not my efforts to make things "just right" that matter most. For if we try too hard to keep our wings - and drama - in motion, we may miss the small, comforting, much more important Presence in the manger.

Everyone Loves a Ventriloquist
By Sam Mitchell

Imagine, a poorly disguised King Saul seeks anonymous consult with the Witches of Endor about an upcoming battle. The last necromancer and magician had "mysteriously" disappeared from the kingdom when their powers fell short. You see, soothsaying does not work on demand. Recognizing Saul through his make-up, one of the witches improvises by grabbing the closest inanimate object (which happened to be the wine flask) and begins making it speak. The battle weary and superstitious Saul believes it to be the work of sorcery and evil spirits, but we all know it to be the wiggling of the bottle and the throwing of one's voice. This was the birth of VENTRILOQUISM.

Vengeful for being put on the spot, she then goes on to tell Saul (through the talking wine flask) that his armies will fall and that he and his sons will be cast into the abode of the dead. And guess what, she was right. Next battle, Saul's armies are defeated and as a direct result he kills himself. King Saul – 0 – Witches of Endor – 1. This story only quickens the gut feeling that I had many Christmases ago: Ventriloquism will betray you.

It was November 1985. I was sitting on the floor of my grandparent's living room. While my parents talked politics with Granny and Pop, I perused the middle section of the holy tome that was known as the Sears Catalog Wish Book.

I scanned each page carefully even though I had no idea what I was looking for. I thought that I was growing too old for the menagerie of stuffed animals that I called close friends. I had yet to bridge my adolescence with wish list items that may have been more age appropriate for a child in the Deep South such as a camouflage tent, duck boots, or even a .22 rifle. At most, I was a budding 7-year-old artist in a 9-year old's body.

Somewhere between Cabbage Patch Dolls and Gobots, something caught my eye. The callout was huge. "Can you say, 'It's Howdy Doody time' without moving your lips?"

OF COURSE, I CAN DO THAT!

This may have been the thing I was looking for, so I kept reading.

"Everyone Loves a Ventriloquist! Pick your favorite character and become the life of the party. Instruction booklet included."

Later, I would question my desire for this awkward toy. Through the muffled bedroom door, I could hear my father's many interesting questions for my Mom about my Christmas list. I could also hear my Mom's verbal melee in defense of me expressing myself creatively. Aware of their different parenting styles, my 9-year-old self would have known to direct these questions to the more responsible party, SEARS.

ME: Dear SEARS, why are you selling Charlie McCarthy dolls to the children of the 80s?

SEARS: Market research shows us that kids genuinely love the same Vaudeville characters as their grandparents.

Christmas morning, 6 AM. I run down the stairs, wake my parents, and make quick work of the wrapping paper that's keeping me from my gifts. I finally made it to the long, rectangular box that held my new, more mature pal. I opened the box more slowly than the others to savor this important moment. With the front flap pulled down, I saw it. It was a vinyl headed, dead-eyed doll laid neatly in its own cardboard coffin. In an instant, I felt that I had betrayed my worn and familiar stuffed friends who sat waiting loyally for me on my bedspread. I gingerly closed the flap and placed the heavy box back on the floor behind me. Although a smile was placed on my face, my true feelings were still handsomely gift wrapped in paper and sealed with scotch tape.

After I thanked them, my parents went back to bed and I went to my room to play with my new gifts. As I sat on my bedroom rug, I fanned out each present from left to right in order of appreciation. The dummy had not even made it to the sprawl. Curiosity finally bested me and I unboxed the toy. If the blank stare from the painted eyes hadn't clued me in to why I felt so queasy, then the blonde hair should have. All of the family coming over later that day for our traditional lasagna lunch had dark hair or at one time in the past had dark hair. This Devil Doll with a head of yellow was some sort of Rolf type from the *Sound of Music*. He may have been in love with Liesl, but he was fated to RAT OUT the entire von Trapp family. One good thing about stuffed animals is that their fur color had never been a point of derision.

I had always carefully named each of my stuffed animals. Kinderly, Cubbie, and Big Eyed Dog had all quickly become part of an adoptive network. We may not have been related, but by God, we were family. I dared not name this new character, for I knew he would not be staying.

Although this oversized, hinged-mouth abomination made me feel physically ill, I knew that soon my family would be here and they would want a performance. I had to practice. I pulled the figure to me, slid my arm inside the cadaver and then began speaking through clenched teeth.

Family arrived. Lasagna was eaten. Manischewitz put way. I reluctantly brought out the dummy for my visiting relatives, tried on a voice and then realized, in front of a live audience that this gift mirrored my uneasiness of outgrowing my childhood things.

After lunch, I snuck the dummy into an opaque garbage bag with the ripped wrapping paper, ribbons and other boxes. Even though my dad didn't see me do this, I'm sure that if he had, he would have been politely silent.

I spent at least one more year playing with my stuffed animals before they made their short journey into our attic.

Perhaps most children who are given ventriloquist dummies are destined to sneak them into the garbage when their parents aren't looking. Maybe Sears was obligated to sell these antiquated toys due to an ancient contract between their corporate shareholders and the Witches of Endor.

But nevertheless, when you are home next holiday, after your presents have been opened, your wine drunk and your lasagna eaten; if it is an option, make your way into your attic, find your old stuffed animals, look at them directly in their cute button eyes and thank them for standing beside you on your path to growing up.

© Sam Mitchell

The Christmas Tree
by Judy Cameron

In spite of World War Two raging in faraway places, my mother somehow was managing our rationing coupons so that nearly every day the special aromas of treats in the oven reminded us that Christmas was near. But the one very different thing added excitement this year: My mother announced that my big brother Ralph, who was in the Army Air Corps, had been granted a furlough and would soon be home from his station in England.

The big double doors to our front parlor were always kept closed, I suppose, to avoid heating it during the cold Wisconsin winter. But when the fragrance of Evergreen seeped into the hall, my brother Ronnie and I lay down on the floor to try to peek through the cracks. We couldn't see anything but cold, balsam laden air hit our faces. We stood up and Ronnie solemnly announced, "It's the North Pole in there!", and I believed him because he was one of my seven big brothers. And sure enough, on Christmas Eve when we returned from church, the parlor doors were open to a breathtaking sight. It was a huge tree decorated with big colored lights and a glorious assortment of things, from glass ornaments to childishly crafted baubles and icicles artfully hung one by one. On the top, stood a big red spire, which my father called God's finger. I don't remember what I got for Christmas that year, but I never will forget that tree.

Most years our trees stayed up until Epiphany, which is January 6th. But this year it wasn't taken down on schedule. Ralph had not come home. We didn't know why, but my mother cheerfully insisted that he would be walking in the back door at any moment to see that beautiful tree. And so it sat in our parlor.

When we passed in the hall, we became aware of the effect of our footsteps. First, a gentle rain of needles, then torrents. My father no longer plugged in the lights. Finally, ornaments began to slide down the bare branches. A couple of them fell during the night, exploding on the hardwood floor and scaring us awake. Mother took a spool of thread from her sewing box and tied the ornaments to the tree. No arguments from my older brothers and sisters could convince my steadfast mother to remove that grotesque skeleton in the parlor.

Our lives moved apprehensively into gray February. Then one morning around Valentine's Day when we woke up, there he was, sitting at the foot of the bed. He smelled like wet wool. Through my sleepy eyes, I recognized the olive drab uniform. "I know who you are!" I said. He laughed, "I know who you are, too." "Did you see the Christmas tree?" He smiled, a broad, satisfied smile. "Yup," he said, "It sure is beautiful."

© Judy Cameron

Two Men and a Hospital Gift Cart
By Rosalind Fellwock

When those two men, wearing their Christmas gear, walked into the office, I knew I was in for an entertaining report of duties completed. These two had been partners on the Gift Cart since they paid their dues and joined the hospital's auxiliary. First came Jim, showing a big grin, bearing the money box for the Finance Desk. He wore his red volunteer jacket topped with a red Santa hat. Then came Charlie with the Santa Hat, Santa jacket, and a pair of red oversized trousers with the ties at the waist hanging below his knees. Charlie was carrying a pillow and looked beat. He muttered, "Boss Lady, I need a much bigger pillow next year, 'cause this one kept falling down to my knees!" Jim and I laughed, but no laugh from Charlie, the skinny Santa.

Then Jim told about one unusual visit as they made their rounds to the wards of this huge medical complex.

"We went into the first room on the fifth floor, checked the name on the door, and greeted Mrs. Howard with our HO-HO-HOs. She looked at our cart and then at us with misery in her eyes, and gave us no smile. She almost whispered, 'I don't think you have anything that can help me.' Charlie said, 'Well, Mrs. Howard, give us a try.' She moaned, 'Fellas, I'm constipated. I need an enema.

"We were speechless for a moment, as we'd never had a request like that. But Charlie recovered faster than I did and he said, 'Jim and I are giving you a free paper to read while we trot down to tell the nursing station that you need something we don't have on our cart today.'

"He reached into his pants pocket and handed me some change for the till, and I gave her a paper. Charlie was groping for his pillow which had fallen to his knees again, and he turned to her and said, 'You see, Mrs. Howard, old Santa has some problems also!' She looked as he tucked the pillow up high and tightened his pants' belt. That did it! She grinned and said 'Thank you as we waved to her and went to the next patient's door." Charlie chimed in, 'Oh yes, we did stop at the nursing station and report her problem.'"

I looked at the two men and said, "You made my day, guys!" I got up from my desk, and gave each of them a hug and said, "Well, being that neither of you bachelors have someone at home to fix supper for you tonight, I will reward you for your duties performed so loyally. Here are two dinner passes for the cafeteria. Enjoy your meal! And Charlie, Jim and I will see that next Christmas, you have a really FAT pillow around your middle!"

With wide smiles, they accepted the passes, stepped into our closet, ridded themselves of their holiday garments, and then waved at me as they went out the door, shouting, "Merry Christmas, Boss Lady!"

© Rosalind Fellwock

(Rosalind Fellwock passed away January 27, 2022, as this book was going to press. She gave many years of support to many local writers, and others, and Roz is missed by all.)

The Red Scooter
by Kathryn Tucker Windham

When I was growing up, down in Thomasville, a little girl, I still believed FIRMLY in Santa Clause. The Christmas that I was maybe 6 years old, the ONLY thing I wanted was a scooter. The only person in Thomasville that had a scooter was my friend, Edith Pritchard, who was a little bit older than I was. She had a scooter but she was kind of stingy about letting you ride her scooter. And the only place you could ride the scooter in Thomasville was on a paved sidewalk was around the Methodist church. She'd bring her scooter to the Methodist church and say, "You can ride around once or twice but don't you drop my scooter and don't you skin it up. Don't you put any scratches on my scooter!" I just resented all those restrictions that were being put on us and I thought, "Well, that's ok. I'm gonna get my own scooter at Christmas time." That's all that I wanted. But I didn't tell anybody that I wanted a scooter.

Well, Christmas morning, I waked up and looked over to where I'd hung my stocking by the fireplace and it was silhouetted against the fire in the grate there. It had bulges and bumps all in it so I knew it had some surprises in it - that I didn't get ashes and switches as some people thought I should've gotten. I explored the stocking and then my daddy came in and said, "I built a fire in the living room and I think it's warm enough now. Let's go see what Santa Clause brought."

So I went in there to see what he'd brought and under that wonderful Cedar Christmas tree were all kinds of surprises for me but there wasn't a scooter. Well, I tried to be happy with what I had but it was obvious I was disappointed. Somebody said, "What's the matter?" and I said, "Santa Clause didn't bring my scooter."

Well, in a little while, I missed my dad and he came back in the house after a while and I heard him tell my mother, "There's not one in town!" Then, a little while later, I heard him talking on the telephone. We had a telephone on the wall in the dining room there. A nice old telephone. And my mother herded me out so I wouldn't hear the conversation but I did hear him say, "Of course I know it's Christmas! That's why I'm calling you!"

Late that afternoon, when the train came from Selma on its way to Mobile, my Daddy said to me, "Let's go down to the depot and meet the train." We often did that because there wasn't much other entertainment in Thomasville. And that cold winter night, that cold Christmas night, I put on my little coat and mittens and cap and took my father's hand and we walked down to the depot.

We went in there by a big old pot-bellied stove that was red hot and people standing around it talking about Christmas and other things. We heard the train blow for Findley's crossing and then for the Double Deck and my father said to me, "Let's move out and stand by the tracks and see who comes and goes." So I walked out with him. We didn't stop where we usually stopped to check on the passengers on the train. He said, "Let's walk down a little bit farther." So we walked a little farther down the track. The train came in and stopped and we were right by the baggage coach. And the door to that baggage coach opened. There was a man standing there and he was holding a red scooter. And he said, "Is your name Kathryn?" I said, "Yes, sir." And he said, "Well, Santa Clause made a bad mistake. He meant to bring you this scooter and he put it off up at Alberta and he asked me to stop by and get it and bring it on down here to you."

Well he handed it out to me and it was the most beautiful red scooter I'd ever seen in my life. And that cold winter night, my father and I went to the Methodist church and I rode my red scooter around and around that church as many times as I wanted to. And it was one of the most wonderful Christmas gifts I ever got.

© Kathryn Tucker Windham

The History of Sundial

Back in the spring of 1984, none of us realized history was being made when Sundial first took to the airwaves on WLRH. It was born out of Judy Watters'

drive to bring music and whatever else she could conjure up to establish a relationship with her audience, a community as varied as cotton farmers to rocket scientists and everything in between. It began as a four-hour program and that's a lot of airtime to fill. In its earliest days Wayne Blackwell was her cohort, though he downplays his role to muse saying it was she who had the vision. The two had a very easy repartee. They interviewed guests from all walks of life: local artists of every stripe, celebrities, musicians in town to play in the symphony. Our astute hostess had an innate ability to, ever so gently, ask the right questions and pry out confidences all the while with a smile in her voice we listeners found charming.

They set phones ringing when Wayne invited their audience to call in and suggest a name for his newborn daughter. After about three years he regretfully bowed out being too busy with his growing family plus a full-time job. And at that point Judy's husband, Harry, stepped up to take his place. He'd already been helping her behind the scenes, pulling the music and contributing ideas. He was the obvious choice. But Harry, ever sensitive to keeping Judy in the forefront, created an exit strategy for himself. Should Judy not like this new arrangement she had only to put a black marble on his pillow and he'd bow out gracefully without recriminations. That cemented the union. It was obvious to listeners that they were a highly compatible unit with the same sense of humor and zest for life's quirks.

Judy had started early with writers Kathryn Tucker Windham, Patricia Sammon, Beth Thames, Margaret Vann and Sara McDaris and over time she collected a stable of friends who happen to be writers. She dreamt up contests, sometimes imposing a particular phrase to be incorporated in their stories. Frequently the show had a theme and on occasion they'd be away from the studio on location. Harry settled in and found his own niche with Little Word Trails that were worthy of a booklet. Most of all, they drew us all into their world where the ether was intoxicating. In those early days much of it was live which left the door wide open to ad hoc, off-the-cuff happenings and flying by the seat of their pants. There were times when Sundial writers performed on air so nerves on edge, every slip, splutter and giggle was heard. Drop-ins brought their children and pets for support. It seemed like Judy and Harry thrived on the unplanned moments that offered the serendipitous spice of uncertainty.

Too many treasured contributors have gone now but there remain several of the very earliest who brought opinions and experiences that gave us all thought. Sundial Writers Corner became a favorite feature of the program. Even when Sundial was reduced to two hours there was always a forum for new poets or essayists to air their pieces.

For years we'd tune in to spend what felt like time with friends. It made a village out of a community of disparate people. This area of North Alabama is made up mostly of people from somewhere else but we felt a kinship on Saturday mornings. On that busy day "driveway moments" were commonplace for Tennessee Valley listeners, when we paused long enough to feel someone's joys or pain.

Sadly, the day came in 2000 when we heard of Harry's demise. He'd shared his illness with his fans. Still, it was shocking to realize what we'd all lost. Judy took a pause and came back later with Morning Blend a few days each week and she made sure to keep her Sundial writers waiting in the wings to be reinstated. They came back strong enough to be heard and Judy did it all.

I was invited to join this group sometime around 2007. I'm vague about it because I was too busy living it to make note of that important date. But I'm very aware what a privilege it is, from coming to the studio to tape, to being in Judy's circle of friends. Meeting so many wonderful, like-minded people has been a major blessing in my life. Judy produced each reading in its entirety from her introduction of each writer, editing and segueing in just the right music. And her call for more submissions never ceased. She was always ready to hear of some new talent to encourage. It became a tour de force to keep track of everyone and give each an opportunity to shine.

By 2018 Judy was beginning to give retirement some thought but then her sister became ill and she flew west to help out. So, though Dorsy recovered well, Judy in fact never went back to work. Now we can only draw on our own memory to imagine her signature sign off, "It's been a pleasure," and know the pleasure was all ours.

Sundial has morphed over thirty-eight years to its

current Monday feature. Dorrie Nutt and Brett Tannehill are eager to keep the current group of almost a hundred writers going. We writers who are blessed with this remarkable platform thank Dorrie and Brett, and particularly you wonderful listeners who give us three minutes of your very busy Mondays. Like the Velveteen Rabbit, we are made real by your love and attention, three minutes at a time, once a week. Please keep giving us that very precious gift. And stay tuned to WLRH.

Joyce Billingsley

About the Cover Artist

Devona Hawkins is a native Huntsvillian who has been harassing the citizens, wildlife, and landscape of North Alabama ever since she was given a Kodak  Instamatic as a child. Her love of nature and all things creative led her to watercolor painting and photography with lesser explored perspectives. Her love of learning and sharing information with others fanned the flames of her macro photography, as well as leading her to beekeeping, heavily documented on her social media outlets.

You can see her most recent work on Instagram @devohawk3, or on Meta/Facebook @DevonaHawkinsPhotography. Her photos and art are available for sale at https://devona-hawkins.square.site/.

Photo of Devona courtesy of Mike Wilson.

Acknowledgements

First, last and always, Dorrie Nutt and Brett Tannehill are the patron saints of the *Sundial Writers Corner*, furnishing the airtime, scheduling reading times, coaching terrified writers into on-air readers, and making our mumblings sound good. And, oh yeah, keeping North Alabama's premier radio platform on the air. Every hour, every day, WLRH fights the good fight of building community and making our lives stronger and more beautiful every day. Thank you both for allowing me to publish the wonderful stories you've worked so hard to collect and feature.

Devona Hawkins took a hundred unreasonable demands from the editor and turned them into a beautiful cover incorporating themes of time and season, diversity and viewpoint, and — oh, yes, a totally impossible demand to add forty-two names to the cover, without ruining the aesthetic she had worked so hard to achieve.

Three editors, Pamala Dempsey, Patricia Guillebeau, and Sarah Sledge gave time and talent to help our writers look their best. You'uns are the best ever.

Thanks also to Charles Dempsey, Mary Guillebeau, Joyce Billingsley, and Madeline Rathz for assistance too varied and valuable to categorize.

But mostly, thanks to the forty-two writers who had the courage to show us their individual memories and dreams, whether those visions were raw or beau-

tiful, funny or achingly painful. Working with broth-
ers and sisters you did not even know you had, you
gave your very vivid and distinct colors to transform
the pale outline of this troubled year into a beautiful,
insightful portrait of our home. I have been honored
and awed to work with each of you.

Michael Guillebeau, Senior Editor

The Care and Feeding of Writers

Writers write to affect readers, and to be affected by them.

If you are affected by anything here, please tell your writer. If you post a review that is both honest and favorable on Amazon, or Goodreads, or Barnes and Noble, then every potential reader for near-eternity will have a reason to read our words.

And we writers will thank you, and cherish your precious, precious review over and over, and probably tattoo the best ones on our chests. If you will take my word for this, I promise not to pull up my shirt to prove it to you.

And, if the book moves you, you can help the writer and your community by going to your local library and request that they put the book on their shelves for other people to enjoy.

But you have already done the most important thing for the care and feeding of the writers here. You have read our words, and allowed us to show you our hearts.

Thank you

Made in the USA
Las Vegas, NV
29 March 2022

46519910R00218